SUICIDE IN AMERICAN INDIANS

SUICIDE
IN AMERICAN INDIANS

David Lester

Nova Science Publishers, Inc.
New York

Art Director: Maria Ester Hawrys
Assistant Director: Elenor Kallberg
Graphics: Susan. Boriotti and Frank Grucci
Manuscript Coordinator: Phyllis Gaynor
Book Production: Gavin Aghamore, Joanne Bennette, Michele Keller
Christine Mathosian and Tammy Sauter
Circulation: Iyatunde Abdullah, Cathy DeGregory and Annette Hellinger

Library of Congress Cataloging-in-Publication Data
available upon request

ISBN 1-56072-429-3

 Nova Science Publishers, Inc.
6080 Jericho Turnpike, Suite 207
Commack, New York 11725
Tele. 516-499-3103 Fax 516-499-3146
E-mail: Novascience@earthlink.net

Printed in the United States of America

Contents

Chapter 1

INTRODUCTION

The problem of suicidal behavior in American Indians is of concern to mental health professionals and public policy makers for two reasons. The first is that frequent suicidal behavior in a community is often taken to be an indicator that social conditions are very bad in that community. Naroll (1963, 1969) suggested that evaluations of a culture could legitimately be made based on the observation of the behaviors of that culture and that suicide was an ideal yardstick for such evaluations. Naroll felt that the relative rarity of suicide made it unlikely to be a "safety valve" for the society (unlike behaviors such as drunkenness), and thus a high suicide rate would not lower the total frustration level of the culture.

Naroll's suggestion has merit (Lester, 1995). When an individual commits suicide, we often do render a negative judgment about that individual and occasionally about the members of the suicide's family. Similarly negative judgments are made on the basis of a high suicide rate in the society as a whole. When people discover that Hungary has had the highest suicide rate of all nations for several decades, they often inquire about the pathological features of Hungary. President Eisenhower used the high suicide rates in Sweden and Denmark to argue against the benefits of socialist policies.

Thus, the documentation of a high suicide rate among some American Indian tribes and on some American Indian reservations serves as a warning sign to us that conditions, both societal and personal, are very bad in those communities.

Secondly, the long history of oppression of the American Indian by the dominant culture has led to concern among policy makers about the present welfare of American Indians. The government has several agencies concerned with American Indians (including the Indian Health Service and the Bureau of Indian Affairs), and these agencies reflect the concern of the society with the social and personal conditions of American Indians.

This book is designed to review what we know at the present time about suicidal behavior in American Indians, what steps have been taken to prevent suicide in these communities, to make suggestions as to how we might better understand suicidal behavior among American Indians and to make recommendations as to how suicide prevention efforts might be focused in the future.

To place this problem in a broader context, it is important to note that other nations have experienced similarly high suicide rates in their aboriginal groups, including Australia (Hunter, 1991), Brazil (Cottle, 1991) and Greenland (Thorslund, 1990). Canada, too, has been concerned with the high rate of suicide in some Canadian aboriginal groups, and data from Canada will be included in the present discussion.

TERMINOLOGY

A brief word is warranted about the terminology used in the present book. There are alternative terms to use when discussing American Indians -- in particular the use of the term "Native Americans" in place of "American Indians." The various tribes have several names by which they are called, and some tribes have strong preferences as to which term they prefer -- such as Inuit rather than Eskimo.

The present book does not seek to make any political statements by its choice of terms, nor to offend any particular group. There is a need, however, to use a standard terminology so that readers can be certain about which group is being discussed. One of the most comprehensive sets of terms is provided by Waldman (1985) in his *Atlas of the North American Indian*. As a consequence I have used his terms. All labels used by others have been converted to the terms used in Waldman's *Atlas* where possible. Subgroups of the major tribes are indicated by (). On a few occasions, it was not possible to locate the particular tribe discussed in a scholarly paper in Waldman's list of tribes. In these cases, the tribe's name as used by the scholar has been placed in [].

Before beginning our review of suicidal behavior in American Indians, it will be useful to review briefly the history of American Indians.

THE DEMOGRAPHIC HISTORY OF AMERICAN INDIANS

American Indians are genetically similar to Asian Mongoloids and arrived from Asia, probably crossing from Siberia to Alaska in several migratory waves from 10,000 to 40,000 years ago. Estimates of the aboriginal population of North America in 1492 range from 900,000 (Kroeber, 1939) to 18 million (Dobyns, 1983). Thornton (1987) suggests 5 million for the USA and 2 million for Canada (out of a world population of about 330 million to 540 million). Estimates of their life expectancy back then range from 19 to 43.

The American Indian population decreased from 5 million to about 250,000 in 1900 for several reasons (Thornton, 1987; Snipp, 1992).

(i) An increased death rate due to diseases brought by European settlers, such as smallpox, measles, cholera, diphtheria, and pneumonia.

(ii) Warfare and genocide, particularly for some tribes such as the Cherokee.

(iii) Removal and relocation from one geographic area to another, especially after the Indian Removal Act of 1830, with high death rates in transit.

(iv) Relocation often split tribes, so that, for example, the Seminole are to be found in Florida and Oklahoma, and combined tribes that were unrelated, such as the Shoshoni and Arapaho on the Wind River Reservation in Wyoming.

(v) These practices, together with European influences (particularly from missionaries), destroyed American Indian ways of life.

(vi) The destruction of their environment, especially the buffalo (from 60 million in aboriginal times to less than 1,000 by 1900) hastened the social and cultural collapse.

(vii) A decrease in fertility as a result of the new diseases, forced migrations, and intermixture with European mates.

THE RESERVATION SYSTEM

The isolation and concentration of American Indians began quite early but was legally justified by the Indian Removal Act of 1830. After passage of this act, many tribes located east of the Mississippi River were relocated to the west of the river. The Iroquois (Seneca), for example, were moved from New York to Oklahoma. Those tribes which did not move, such as the Ojibway in Wisconsin, had much of their territory confiscated (Snipp, 1992).

As the Anglo population migrated westwards, the tribes west of the Mississippi River were forced to give up much of the land that had been granted to them, both those native to the region such as the Sioux, and those newly moved there such as the Cherokee. The reservations usually were situated on the least desirable land, with few natural resources, and far removed from major urban areas.

The policy then changed toward forcing the American Indians to assimilate, and the Dawes Act of 1887 permitted the land controlled by American Indians to be split into small parcels and given to individual American Indians, with the aim of turning them into ranchers and farmers. In 1953, legislation was passed to remove reservations from their status as independent political entities and to start employment and relocation programs to encourage American Indians to leave reservations for other parts of the United States. This approach was soon abandoned. However, whereas in 1930 only 10% of American Indians lived in urban areas, by 1970 this percentage had risen to 48% (Gundlach, et al., 1977). Some 20% of American Indians in 1970 claimed no tribal identity and more than a third of American Indian men had married white wives as compared to only 2% of African American men.

Since 1950, the proportion of American Indians living on reservations has declined from roughly 50% to about 25% by 1980. In 1980, 336,384 American Indians lived on reservations and about 14% of all American Indians lived on reservations with poverty rates of 40% or more (Sandefur, 1989). Sandefur identified ten reservations with poverty rates of 40% or higher and female headship rates of 30% or higher, and a further eight reservations with poverty rates of 40% or higher but female headship rates of less than 30%. Eighteen of the 36 largest reservations (that is, with populations over 2,000) met the criteria for being "underclass," that segment of the poor whose situation seems relatively immune to economic conditions and social programs designed to help.

To counter this poverty, programs exist to educate the youth so that they can more easily move into the mainstream society, and efforts are being made to develop the economies on the reservation through the exploitation of natural resources or the establishment of businesses, such as casinos.

Although there is much to criticize about conditions on the reservations, many American Indians are content to remain there, for the reservations do permit the maintenance of a cultural base for the tribes, where the native language can be spoken and traditional ways followed. There is a strong sense of family and community, and social services are provided on the reservations administered by the tribal governments.

The Twentieth Century

The American Indian population has grown during this century, particularly since 1950. Thornton (1987) gives the following numbers:

1890	248,253
1900	237,196
1910	276,927
1920	244,437
1930	343,352
1940	345,252
1950	357,499
1960	523,591
1970	792,730
1980	1,366,676

The reasons for this increase in recent years include;

(i) A high birth rate. The birth rate for American Indians peaked in 1964 at 43 per 1,000 people. In 1971 it was 33 as compared to a rate of 18 in the USA as a whole. The number of children ever born to 1,000 women aged 15 to 44 was 1687 for American Indian women in 1980 as compared to 1302 for the USA as a whole.

(ii) The declining death rate among American Indians. In 1980 the death rate was 5.0 per 1000 for American Indians as compared to 8.7 for the USA as a whole. (The infant mortality rate, however, has been higher for American Indians than for the USA as a whole, though the difference has been decreasing in recent years.)

(iii) Changes in the definition and enumeration of American Indians. Prior to 1960, census observers noted whether they believed a person to be an American Indian or not. Since 1960, self-reporting has been used. Many American Indian tribes now set criteria for defining a member. For example, the Cherokee Nation of Oklahoma in its constitution developed in the 1970's set no minimum blood quantity for tribal membership. One must merely trace one's descent along Cherokee lines.

Simmons (1977) has listed six ways in which American Indians may be defined: (1) *legal definitions*, such as being a member of a tribe, (2) *self-declaration*, (3) *community recognition* by other Indians, (4) *recognition by non-Indians*, (5) *biological definitions*, such as blood mixture, and (6) *cultural definitions*, such as acting as Indians should.

URBANIZATION

Since 1950, there has been a large scale movement of American Indians to urban areas. Thornton (1987) has provided estimates of the percentage of urbanized American Indians:

1890	0.0%
1900	0.4%
1910	4.5%
1920	6.1%
1930	9.9%
1940	7.2%
1950	13.4%
1960	27.9%
1970	44.5%
1980	49.0%

This urbanization has had three consequences: a declining birth rate among the urban American Indians, more intermarriage, and reduced tribal importance. In 1980, over half of all American Indians were married to non-Indians as compared to about one percent of whites and two percent of blacks. Thus, in the future, genetic definitions of who is an American Indian may make less sense than definition in terms of descent.

CANADA

The situation of Canadian Indians is perhaps even worse than that of American Indians. Ward, et al. (1978) and Kirmayer (1994) have documented their situation with some striking statistics. By 1994 there were 596 bands of Indians in Canada with access to 2,284 reserves. The average size of the band has grown from about 200 to about 500. In the 1970's about 70% of status Indians lived on the reserves, and they numbered about 300,000. In addition, non-status Indians, or Métis, (most of whom have married non-Indians) numbered about 600,000. There are also some 17,000 Eskimos, though they prefer the label "Inuit." Four hundred years ago, there were perhaps about 250,000 Canadian Indians. By the beginning of this century, the number was down to about 100,000, and the number rose to about one million by the 1970's.

The birth rate of Canadian Indians is higher and the life expectancy lower than for white Canadians. Education is poor and illiteracy common. Housing for status Indians is poor -- crowded and often without adequate water and sewage facilities.

Ward, et al. characterize the Canadian government policy as a plan to absorb the Indian culture into the dominant white culture. The government was paternalistic, though well-meaning, leaving the Indians out of the planning for their lives. The reserve system isolated them from the dominant culture, yet the laws restricted their traditional life style, and the social service system impaired their motivation and self-concept. Their language, customs, knowledge and religion were mocked. The Indian could stay on the reservation, face unemployment and the lack of a meaningful life, or migrate to the slums of the cities where they would face racial discrimination and unemployment. Ward noted that it is an indictment of the reservation system that so many Indians chose the city slums instead. Ninety percent of the Indians families live below the poverty level.

Ward gives the example of the Wikwemikong Indian Reservation in Northern Ontario where the Indians had farmed since the 1800's. They could not afford modern machinery and were still using horses to pull their equipment, while neighboring white farmers were using tractors. By the 1950's, they were no longer farming, most of the families were on welfare, and alcohol abuse was rampant.

Prior to World War Two, Indian children were sent to religious boarding schools for education. The teachers were second-rate, and they imposed white culture on the Indian pupils. They alienated the children from their own culture, turned them against the white culture, and provided no skills useful for their later lives. In the 1950's, the government took over the education, and its failure is documented by the fact that 94 percent of Indians do not graduate from high school. (Ward noted that Indian parents contribute to this by not exerting more pressure on their children to attend and excel at school -- the parents are very permissive with their children and demand little of them.) In the last thirty years, Ward noted that only 525 Indians had achieved a university education. Twenty-four percent of the Indians are illiterate.

Some twenty-five percent of all prisoners are Canadian Indians, even though they constitute a minute proportion of the population. Most are imprisoned for petty crimes -- armed robbery or kidnapping are rare.

COMMENT

This introductory chapter has explained why suicide in American Indians is of great concern to public health professionals and policy makers. Some data have also been presented on the demographic history of the American Indian and the Canadian Indian so that the information of suicide presented later can be seen in the context of the socioeconomic characteristics of the American and Canadian Indian population.

REFERENCES

Cottle, M. Cowboys and Indians, 1994. *Mother Jones*, 1994, 19(4), 16.

Dobyns, H. F. *Their number thinned.* Knoxville: University of Tennessee, 1983.

Gundlach, J. H., Reid, P. N., & Roberts, A. E. Migration, labor mobility, and relocation assistance. *Social Service Review*, 1977, 51, 464-473.

Hunter, E. M. An examination of recent suicides in remote Australia. *Australian & New Zealand Journal of Psychiatry*, 1991, 25, 197-202.

Kirmayer, L. J. Suicide among Canadian aboriginal peoples. *Transcultural Psychiatric Research Review*, 1994, 31, 3-58.

Kroeber, A. L. Cultural and native areas of native North America. *University of California Publications in American Archaeology and Ethnology*, 1939, 38, 1-242.

Lester, D. Thwarting disorientation and suicide: An examination of Naroll's theory of suicide. *Cross-Cultural Research*, 1995, 29, 14-26.

Naroll, R. Thwarting disorientation and suicide. Unpublished paper, Northwestern University, 1963.

Naroll, R. Cultural determinants and the concept of the sick society. In S. C. Plog & R. B. Edgerton, (Eds.) *Changing perspectives in mental illness*. New York: Holt, Rinehart & Winston, 1969, 128-155.

Sandefur, G. D. American Indian reservations: the first underclass areas? *Focus*, 1989, 12(1), 37-41.

Simmons, J. L. One little, two little, three little Indians. *Human Organization*, 1977, 36, 76-79.

Snipp, C. M. Sociological perspectives on American Indians. *Annual Review of Sociology*, 1992, 18, 351-371.

Thornton, R. *American Indian holocaust and survival*. Norman, OK: University of Oklahoma, 1987.

Thorslund, J. Inuit suicides in Greenland. *Arctic Medical Research*, 1990, 49, 25-33.

Waldman, C. *Atlas of the North American Indian*. New York: Facts on File, 1985.

Ward, J. A., Fox, J., & Evans, A. L. Suicide and the Canadian Indians. In V. Aalberg (Ed.) *Proceedings of the 9th International; Congress of the International Association for Suicide Prevention*. Helsinki, Finland: Finnish Association for Mental Health, 1978, 389-401.

Chapter 2

THE RELIABILITY, VALIDITY AND COMPARABILITY OF AMERICAN INDIAN SUICIDE RATES

One of the first issues we must consider before discussing the rate and pattern of American Indian suicide (in Chapter 3) is whether the data on American Indian suicide are valid. Webb and Willard (1975) argued forcefully that calculated American Indian suicide rates are not valid. They suggested that Anglo suicides are much more likely to be covered up and certified as other-than-suicide because of Anglo cultural values, insurance claims, and denial by the attending physician. The argument that differences in the suicide rates of different groups is a result of differential accuracy in recording the cause of death has been made before. Douglas (1967) argued that this factor could explain, at least in part, such phenomena as gender differences in suicide rates, urban/rural differences, and differences by religion.

Historically, Webb and Willard noted, American Indians did not have a written language and so recording of events was not possible. Later, the early missionaries, colonialists and soldiers were not concerned with making detailed observations of American Indian life, and it was only with the establishment of reservations and the development of a Federal bureaucracy that more complete recording of events was possible.

The small population base for some groups of American Indians makes the suicide rate very sensitive to localized occurrences. For example, with a population of around 600,000 for American Indians as a whole, a spate of nine suicides in one group would raise the overall suicide rate nationally by 1.5. In addition, the migration of American Indians from the reservations to the cities often leads to them dropping out of the American Indian statistics.

In short, Webb and Willard argued that it is meaningless to compare American Indian suicide rates with those of the nation as a whole.

UNDERREPORTING OF AMERICAN INDIAN SUICIDES

Missed Suicides

In contrast to Webb and Willard who argued that white suicides are covered up more often by medical examiners than are American Indian suicides, there are several statistical studies indicating that American Indian suicides are underreported. Marshall and Soule (1988) examined deaths in 49 Native villages in southwest Alaska for the period 1979-1984. They found five suicides recorded in the Alaska Department of Health and Social Services (and, therefore, reported to the Federal Government). However, a search through the coroners' files identified 33 further suicides. Thus, the actual suicide rate was 36.9 per 100,000 per year as compared to the official rate of 7.3. Marshall and Soule attributed this discrepancy to incorrect coding by the National Center for Health Statistics and poor communication between the coroners and higher authorities.

Cooper, et al. (1992) examined coroners' files for Canadian Indians in British Columbia for 1987-1989. Out of 104 deaths classified as homicide, accidental or undetermined, they thought that five were probable suicides. They then compared files for 177 Canadian Indian suicides and 177 suicides in other ethnic groups. They found ten non-Indian cases to be Indians. Although the nature of the coroner's examination was similar for both groups of suicides, these data suggest that suicides in Canadian Indians are undercounted.

Sievers, et al. (1990) reviewed deaths for a community of Pima Indians in Arizona for 1975-1984 and estimated a suicide rate of 53 suicides as compared to the official rate of 49.

A report from Ontario (Anon, 1973) suggests that the undercounting of suicide may be greater for women than for men. From 1970-1973 the authors of the report identified 20 confirmed male suicides and four female suicides. However, there were ten suspected female suicides as compared to only two suspected male suicides.

Missed American Indians

Andress (1977) analyzed suicides in Riverside County (California) from 1965-1969 and found two American Indian suicides which had been reported as Mexican American. Previously, the county had reported no American Indian suicides. Andress noted that two factors contributed to this ethnic misclassification: (1) the fact that many American Indians in California have Mexican surnames, and (2) only about 40% of the American Indians live on the reservations, making location of the suicide an unreliable variable for deciding upon ethnic group.

Sugarman, et al. (1993) reported data that support this, but in a study on accidental deaths. In Oregon in 1989-1990 they identified 301 American Indians who died from injuries or who were hospitalized for at least one day. However, when they compared the list of such people with names contained in the Indian Health Service files, they identified 89 more American Indians in their original sample. The likelihood of an American Indian patient not being recorded as such was higher for men, those with less than 25% blood quantum and those in metropolitan areas.

Disguised Suicides

It has often been argued that many suicidal deaths are misrecorded as from other causes because of the difficulty of deciding upon the "true" cause. For example, some people act in such a way as to increase the risk that another will murder them, *victim-precipitated homicide*, and this behavior has been seen as motivated, at least in part, by suicidal impulses.

Mindell and Stuart (1968) noted that many American Indians die in accidents, especially car crashes, from alcohol abuse, and from refusing medical treatment and advice, and many of these deaths may be suicides or at least motivated in part by suicidal impulses. LaFromboise and Bigfoot (1988) also noted that the use of cars for suicide by American Indians may lead to an undercount, more so than in the general population since car deaths are common among American Indians. For example, in 1975-1977, the age-adjusted death rate from motor vehicles for American Indians was 152.5 per 100,000 per year, seven times the American rate (May, 1987). Fatal single car crashes may be suicides but are deaths which will be typically be classified as accidental.

PATTERNS OF SUICIDE

Webb and Willard (1975) argued that scholars should take care not to generalize from one group of American Indians to another. In a brief review of some of the literature on suicide in American Indians, they describe six very different patterns.

(1) Among the Shoshoni (Western) Indians, now living on small reservations in Idaho, Nevada and Wyoming, the estimated rate may be as high as 100 per 100,000 per year, about ten times the national average. This high rate seems to be generated by the suicides of young males who drop out of school, get into difficulties with the law, and abuse alcohol and other drugs. Family disorganization and unemployment may also play a role.

(2) The Pueblo Indians (Webb and Willard did not specify which of the eight major subgroups they were referring to) have managed to keep many of their traditions despite some acculturation, and the more traditional Pueblos appear to have lower suicide rates than the more acculturated ones.

(3) The Sioux (Dakota) and Cheyenne were thought by Webb and Willard to commonly express their self-destructive impulses in "Crazy-Dog"

behavior, in which the individual provokes death from the hands of another, in olden times by attacking others and in more modern times in barroom brawls or by walking across freeways and being hit by cars.

(4) The Papago, Pima and Yaquis (Uto-Aztecan) are reported to have had virtually no suicides in times gone by, with suicide appearing only from the 1960's on. Now young males, usually intoxicated, are the most common victims.

(5) The Apache (White Mountain) have a relatively higher incidence of murder-suicide than the other groups, and the female suicide rate appears to have risen dramatically in recent years.

(6) Finally, the Navajo have kept their culture more intact than many other American Indian groups, and their suicide rate has remained steady since 1900. The most common precipitant is conflict with a kinsman or spouse, and they typically commit suicide near their house. In contrast, most suicide attempts among the Navajo are made by women.

As a result of their brief survey, Webb and Willard stressed that it is not appropriate to generalize from suicidal behavior in one American Indian group to other groups, and certainly not from American culture in general to American Indians. Furthermore, we cannot assume that suicide prevention techniques devised for the general American culture will be useful for American Indians. For example, many American Indian groups feel most uncomfortable talking about feelings to nongroup members, and so a telephone crisis intervention service may not be utilized by American Indians, even if telephones were available in the areas in which they live. This issue will be discussed in greater detail in the chapter on suicide prevention (Chapter 9).

COMMENT

The data presented in this chapter do suggest that reported official rates of suicide in American and Canadian Indians may be underestimates. However, this may be true for other ethnic groups too, but no study has yet compared the under-reporting of suicide for different ethnic groups -- this would, of course, be a most worthwhile study for the future. There are also no data yet on whether the under-reporting of American Indian suicide is more extreme in some tribes than in others. Research on this issue would also be of great interest and importance. Meanwhile, we must view the reported suicide rates which are presented in the following chapters for American Indians as a whole and for each tribe with some caution.

REFERENCES

Andress, V. R. Ethnic/racial misidentification in death. *Forensic Science*, 1977, 9, 179-183.

Anon. *While people sleep*. Kenora, Ontario: Grand Council Treaty #3, 1973.

Cooper, M., Corrado, R., Karlberg, A. M., & Adams, L. P. Aboriginal suicide in British Columbia. *Canada's Mental Health*, 1992, 40(3), 19-23.

Douglas, J. D. *The social meanings of suicide*. Princeton: Princeton University, 1967.

LaFromboise, T. D., & Bigfoot, D. S. Cultural and cognitive considerations in the prevention of American Indian adolescent suicide. *Journal of Adolescence*, 1988, 11, 135-153.

Marshall, D. L., & Soule, S. Accidental deaths and suicides in southwest Alaska. *Alaska Medicine*, 1988, 30(2), 45-52.

May, P. A. Suicide and self-destruction among American Indian youths. *American Indian & Alaska Native Mental Health Research*, 1987, 1(1), 52-69.

Mindell, C., & Stuart, P. Suicide and self-destructive behavior in the Oglala Sioux. *Pine Ridge Research Bulletin*, 1968, 1, 14-23.

Sievers, M. L., Nelson, R. G., & Bennett, P. H. Adverse mortality experience of a southwestern American Indian community. *Journal of Clinical Epidemiology*, 1990, 43, 1231-1242.

Sugarman, J. R., Soderberg, R., Gordon, J. E., & Rivara, F. P. Racial misclassification of American Indians. *American Journal of Public Health*, 1993, 83, 681-684.

Webb, J. P., & Willard, W. Six American Indian patterns of suicide. In N. L. Farberow (Ed.) *Suicide in different cultures*. Baltimore: University Park Press, 1975, 17-33.

Chapter 3

GENERAL PATTERNS OF SUICIDE

In this chapter we will review the data on suicide in American Indians and Canadian Indians in general, irrespective of the particular tribe involved. The data come from studies of the nations as a whole or of particular regions, rather than from particular reservations where the tribal composition is clear.

Havighurst (1971) noted that the suicide rate for American Indians (in the 24 reservation states) for 1959-1966 was 11 per 100,000 per year, about the same as for the USA as a whole (10.8). However, the suicide rate for American Indians was higher among the young (15-44) and among men. American Indian elderly and females were at relatively low risk of suicide as compared to Americans as a whole. Havighurst noted that the young American Indians committing suicide were of relatively low socio-economic status, and so their suicide rates ought to be compared with the suicide rates of lower class white males, whose suicide rates do appear to be higher than for white middle class males according to the studies reported by Havighurst (for example, Maris [1967]).

Havighurst noted that the practice of sending American Indian youth away to boarding school is often mentioned by scholars as a suicidogenic stressor for American Indian youth, but he noted that virtually no suicides had occurred at those schools. He also noted the existence of "suicide epidemics" but, when a longer period of time was examined, the suicide rates were not excessively high. For example, an "epidemic" on the Quinault Indian Reservation in Washington State in 1962-1964 was followed by zero suicides in the next five years. (The issue of whether clusters of suicides exist is discussed further later in this chapter.) Havighurst also noted that extreme variability of suicide rates from tribe to tribe with, for example, the Navajo having an average suicide rate while the Shoshoni [Shoshone-Bannock] at Fort Hall, Idaho, have a high suicide rate.

Ogden, et al. (1970) noted that the American Indian suicide rate showed a dramatic increase in 1967. From 1959 through 1965, the American Indian suicide rate ranged between 11.3 and 12.1. In 1967 it rose to 17.0, jumping from about 1.1:1 as a ratio with respect to the total American suicide rate to 1.6:1. Using age-adjusted suicide rates, the increase was even more dramatic. The American Indian suicide rate from 1959 though 1965 ranged between 15.3 and 17.0, rising to 23.1 in 1967, a ratio of 2.1:1 as compared with the total American suicide rate. The American Indian suicide rate peaked at age 25 to 34 in 1965-1967 as compared to a peak for the ages of 55 to 64 for the total American population. The percentage of suicides which were men was higher in American Indians, 83% for 1959 to 1966 as compared to 74% for the total American population.

Kramer, et al. (1972) looked at suicide rates in the United States for 1959-1961. By ethnic groups the age-adjusted suicide rates were Chinese 21.3, American Indian 14.6, Japanese 11.8, white 11.0, and African American 4.8. White, Chinese and Japanese suicide rates rose with age, the latter two ethnic groups precipitously so, while American Indian suicide rates peaked at age 25-34. In old age, American Indian suicide rates were lower than those of whites. Kramer suggested that the higher suicide rates in the western states of the United States may be, in part, a result of the higher proportion of American Indians and Chinese in these states.

For the late 1960's, May and Dizmang (1974) reported a suicide rate of 23.1 per 100,000 per year for American Indians and Alaska Natives as compared to a rate of 11.1 for the general American population. In a review of research by others, they reported suicide rates in the 1960's ranging from 9.0 for the Navajo to 20.8 for the Apache. Even the Pueblo Indian groups had suicide rates ranging from zero to 22.2. In addition, other forms of self-destructive behavior were common, including accidental deaths and deaths from cirrhosis of the liver as a result of alcohol abuse.

May and Dizmang found suicide to be most common in young male American Indians between the ages of 15 and 39, in contrast with the general population for whom suicide rates rise with age (at least in men). In contrast, the typical American Indian suicide attempter was young and female, not unlike the general population. A large proportion of attempted and completed suicides occurred when the individual had been drinking, but the method used varied greatly from tribe to tribe. The location for the suicide varied a great deal also -- for some tribes occurring near the home, for others in jails.

May and Dizmang noted that both the rate and the pattern of suicide in American Indian tribes could have their roots in the tribes themselves, with both the rate and the pattern staying constant over several hundred years, or the rate and patterns could be recent developments in response to conflicts which have arisen only in recent years.

McIntosh and Santos (1981) looked at suicide rates in 1976, and found that the suicide rate of American Indians (19.2 per 100,000 per year) was higher than the rates for whites (13.3), African Americans (6.5), Chinese Americans (9.1), Japanese Americans (8.6) and Filipino Americans (3.4). With respect to age, American Indians and African Americans both had suicide rates that peaked in youth, 15 to 24 for American Indians and 25 to 34 for African Americans. In contrast, the suicide rates of other ethnic groups in America peaked in old age. For American Indians, the peak had decreased from 1960 to 1976, from 25 to 34 to 15 to 24 year olds.

McIntosh and Santos speculated that the relatively low suicide rate in elderly American Indians might be a result of the esteem in which the leaders are held by American Indians tribes. However, this respect is in danger of eroding over time, and so we might, therefore, expect changes in the age distribution of American Indian suicides. However, an alternative explanation suggested by McIntosh and Santos is that fewer of an American Indian cohort survive into old age than is the case for other ethnic minorities, and so the elderly may be hardier than the average American Indian. Finally, the elderly American Indians do not face the acculturation problems of the young -- the elderly have made their peace with the "two cultures."

Justice (1985) found a crude suicide rate for the regions covered by the Indian Health Service for 1981-1983 of 17.2, peaking for those aged 15 to 24 at 33.9. From 1960 to 1980, the peak suicide rate moved from those aged 25 to 29 to those aged 20 to 24. However, the suicide rate varied greatly from region to region, and even within the regions.

More recently, Hisnanick (1994) has noted that from 1973-1988 the American Indian and Alaska Native suicide has been deceasing (both for men and women), the crude rate by about 2.7% per year and the age-adjusted rate by 2.5%, which is greater than the yearly decrease in the American age-adjusted suicide rate as a whole of 0.6%. The ratio of the male American Indian suicide rate to the female rate has been increasing over the period. Throughout this period, though, the American Indian suicide rate has remained higher than the overall American suicide rate.

ADOLESCENT SUICIDE

Berlin (1987) reviewed the research and data on adolescent suicide in American Indians and drew several conclusions. The majority of suicides are committed by males, primarily by means of shooting and hanging, and almost always when intoxicated. Attempted suicide is primarily a female behavior, accomplished by overdose. The suicides are characterized by loss of caretakers though death or divorce and a long arrest record in both the adolescent and the caretakers. The chaotic home environment which the youths appear to have experienced was seen by Berlin as similar to the pattern described for black and adolescent suicidal youths (Teicher, 1979) and, we might add, youths in general (Jacobs, 1972).

Conclusions

The data from the USA as a whole indicates that the American Indian suicide rate is a little higher than the suicide rate for the general population. This increase, however, is more marked in men than in women and is especially noteworthy in the youth.

Studies on Specific Regions

Alaska

Kraus (1972, 1974; Kraus & Buffler, 1976, 1977) noted that the Alaskan Native suicide rate was 13 in the period, 1961-1965, 25 for 1966-1970, and 29.6 in 1970 (compared to an overall suicide rate in Alaska of 13.2 in 1970). The jump in the suicide rate occurred in 1965, mainly due to the increase in suicide among youths aged 15 to 24. The typical suicide was male, in the age range 15 to 25, and used a gun (compared to the typical attempter who was female, aged 15 to 25, and who used pills). The suicide rate in 1972 was 40.4, with the mean age of the suicides being 23.7 years. The male/female ratio was about 3:1 and, though guns continued to be the most common method for suicide, the use of drug overdoses was increasing in frequency.

Kraus and Buffler (1979) found an outpatient attempted suicide rate in Alaska area native health services ranging from 205 to 302 for 1971-1977. The hospitalized attempted suicide rate varied from 100 to 251 during this period, but there may be some overlap between the patients in these two groups. For the outpatients, the percentage of attempts which were alcohol-related ranged from 37% to 60% over the years.

Forbes and van der Hyde (1988) reported suicide rates for Alaskan Natives for 1978-1985. While the suicide rates for white males and white females declined over this period (from 32.0 to 24.1 for males and from 8.2 to 6.8 for females), the rates for Alaskan Natives increased (from 57.4 to

100.1 for males and from 13.2 to 24.1 for females). The increase was especially notable for Alaska Native males aged 15 to 24 (from 168.1 to 206.6).

Parkin (1974) looked at suicidal behavior in Fairbanks, Alaska, from 1960-1971. In 1960, Fairbanks had a population of 13,311, of whom 245 were Eskimos and 189 American Indians (Aleuts, [Athabascans] and Tlingit/Haida). Parkin characterized the whites as middle-class, the Eskimos as poor and the American Indians as abject poor. Based on Parkin's data, the estimated suicide rate for the Eskimos was 51.9, for the American Indians 21.9 and for the other inhabitants 10.7. During the period studied, 34 Eskimos attempted suicides (mostly women) and two completed suicide; 25 American Indians attempted suicide (mostly women) and one completed suicide; 125 whites attempted suicide (mostly women) and 17 completed suicide. Among the attempters, white women were more likely to use overdoses and less likely to use cutting. Also, the only female attempters using firearms were white. The white female attempters engaged in more lethal suicidal actions but communicated their suicidal intent (both before and after the act) as equally often as the Alaska Native and American Indian women attempters.

Parkin saw suicidal behavior in the whites as resulting from (1) a tendency for the whites moving to Alaska to have a greater incidence of psychiatric disorder than whites in the lower 48 states, (2) the stress from work and social isolation, and (3) depression from being housebound during the winter months. In contrast, suicidal behavior in the American Indians and Eskimos seemed to result from acculturation stress and loss of cultural norms, prejudice, limited job skills and job opportunities, and alcohol abuse. In support of his acculturation hypothesis Parkin found that more of the suicidal American Indians and Eskimos came from villages of less than 500 people than did the nonsuicidal American Indians and Eskimos. Only 9% of the suicidal American Indians and Eskimos came from cities of more than 2500 people whereas 48% of the total population of American Indians and Eskimos lived in such cities.

Parkin noted differences in the suicidal patterns of the American Indians and the Eskimos. The Eskimos had a prohibition against the direct expression of anger and were often depressed. The American Indians, on the other hand, (Parkin here focused on the [Athabascans]) acted out their feelings angrily, manipulatively and impulsively when drunk. Parkin noted that these differences were probably a result of different child-rearing experiences. Child-rearing among the Eskimos is marked by caring, warmth and love; the Athabascans treat their children more coldly and harshly. For example, Eskimo children are handled a lot and play freely while Athabascan children are kept for much of the time in a hammock which can be rocked by the mother.

Kost-Grant (1983) found a suicide rate for Alaska Natives for 1976-1980 of 30.6 compared to a non-Native rate of 16.3. The firearm suicide rates were 24.0 and 13.3 respectively. Thirty four Alaska Natives survived a gunshot wound (five accidental and 29 suicide attempters). The modal survivor was male, intoxicated with alcohol, impulsive and motivated by interpersonal problems with families or romantic attachments, with a mean age 21.4.

Hlady and Middaugh (1987, 1988) examined suicide rates in Alaska for 1983-1984. The suicide rate for whites was 16.5 (25.2 for men and 6.4 for women), whereas the suicide rate for Alaska Natives was 44.2 (73.5 for men and 13.9 for women). The age-adjusted rates were 19.1 for whites and 42.9 for Alaska Natives. The median age for the white suicides was 32 and for the Alaska Natives 23. The suicide rate for Alaska Natives was roughly twice as high in the rural areas than the urban areas 50.5 versus 27.4), whereas the suicide rate of whites was slightly lower in the rural areas (14.4 versus 15.2).

The seasonal distributions of white and Alaska Native suicides were similar (with peaks in the Spring and Fall), and the daily distributions were similar also. The majority of suicides used firearms, and 59% of the suicides were intoxicated with alcohol at the time of their death, but there were no ethnic differences in these factors. Fewer of the Alaska Natives were married, but this was due to their younger age. The white and Alaska Native suicides did not differ in unemployment status.

Kettl and Bixler (1988a, 1988b, 1991) identified 90 suicides among Alaska Natives in the period 1979-1984. The modal suicide was male (the male suicide rate was 38.2 and the female rate 8.5), 15 to 24 years old, using firearms, single (78% of the men and 44% of the women were single; one-third of the women, however, were divorced compared to only 5% of the men), dying between midnight and 4 a.m., and 44% were born in the period of April to July, significantly more than chance would predict and more than Alaskan Natives in general. Those suicides who had been seen at the Alaska Native Medical Center were compared to nonsuicidal natives also seen there. The suicides had more often attempted suicide and abused alcohol, but did not differ in psychiatric diagnosis, psychiatric treatment or medical problems.

It is clear, then, that the suicide rate among Alaska Natives is much higher than that of whites in the state, and this is particularly so for the youth and those in rural areas of Alaska. In addition, alcohol intoxication is very common in those committing suicide.

Canada

Mao, et al. (1992) reported that the suicide rate in 1981 for registered Indians in Canada was 58.6 for men and 16.8 for women. For those on Indian reserves in 1979-1983, the suicide rates were 59.9 and 19.4 respectively.

Anon (1990-1991) reported a suicide rate for Canadian Indians in 1987 of 38.4, 2.7 times higher than the total Canadian suicide rate. For Canadian Indian females, the suicide rate (averaged for 1984-1988) peaked at ages 20 to 29 (for whom the rate was 22.1, 3.6 times the total Canadian rate), but the suicide rate for those aged 10 to 19 (17.3) was 7.5 times the total Canadian suicide rate. For Canadian Indian males, the suicide rate also peaked for those aged 20-29 (at 142.2, 4.6 times the total Canadian suicide rate), while the suicide rate for Canadian Indian males aged 10 to 19 (60.0) was 5.1 times the total Canadian suicide rate. The Canadian Indian suicide rates varied from region to region, being lowest in the Northwest Territories (22.5) and highest in the Yukon (61.9).

Health Canada (1994) reported that the age-adjusted suicide rate for Canadian Indians in 1990 was 22 per 100,000 per year compared to 11 for the population of Canada as a whole. In charts presented for Canada for

1987-1991, Canadian Indians had higher suicide rates for both men and women than Canadians as a whole for all age groups save those over the age of 65. The difference was especially large for males aged 15 to 24, for whom the Indian suicide rate was about 115 compared to an overall Canadian suicide rate of about 25. (The use of charts makes accurate rates impossible to discern from this publication.) Mao, et al. (1986) calculated suicides rates for 1977-1982: age-adjusted rates for Canadian Indians on reserves were 53 for men and 17 for women compared to 19.9 and 6.4 for Canadian men and women in general.

Hislop, et al., (1987) calculated suicides rates for British Columbia for 1953-1978. Canadian Indians had suicide rates of 39.4 for men and 13.1 for women compared to 20.7 and 8.0 for non-Indians. The Canadian Indian suicide rates were higher than those for non-Indians for all age groups save those over the age of 65.

Cooper, et al. (1992) calculated a suicide rate for Canadian Indians in British Columbia in 1984-1989 of between 23.6 and 27.4, which contrasted with a suicide rate of 16.1 for other British Columbians. The rate for reservation Indians was 37 and for non-reservation Indians 16. The rates peaked for men aged 15 to 24 at 90 and for women aged 15 to 24 at 23. The areas with the highest suicide rates for Indians were in central British Columbia. The areas with the lowest rates were in the northwest and southwest of the province, while the major urban centers had rates for Indians similar to those for non-Indians. Tonkin (1984) examined suicides by adolescents aged 15 to 19 in British Columbia in 1978-1979, The Canadian Indians were less often living in the cities, but did not differ in gender, method used or whether they had been drinking from the non-Indian suicides.

Balikci (1960b) reported on 27 cases of completed and attempted suicide among the Eskimos of Pelly Bay in the Northwest Territories of Canada over the last fifty years. The modal suicidal person was a young or middle-aged adult, male, using shooting, hanging or strangulation. Most had consulted with relatives first and committed suicide after a period of collective deliberation. Six people had been discouraged from committing suicide. However, some cases were more impulsive. Nine cases were motivated by an incurable illness, nine cases by the sickness or death of a child, three by tensions between spouses, and two by old age. Despite the planning and discussion preceding suicidal behavior, Balikci saw the suicides as resulting from suppressed anger and a low level of societal integration, both explanations apparently at odds with the description of the suicidal behavior he provided. Balikci (1960a) noted a suicide rate of about 575 among the Netsilik Eskimos of Pelly Bay over a 50 year period earlier this century, with a similar rate of attempted suicide. Hanging was the most popular method, followed by firearms, and the most common motivations were old age and infirmity.

Prince (1988) reported a suicides rate for registered Canadian Indians in 1982-1983 of 39.6. For the Eskimo in the Northwest Territories in 1979-1983 the suicide rate was 35.7. Butler (1965) calculated an Eskimo suicide rate in the Northwest Territories for 1959-1964 of 18.8 (compared to a white suicide rate of 20.0). Canadian Indians in the Northwest Territories had a suicide rate of 0.0 while those in the Yukon had a suicide rate of 37.7 -- rates which averaged out (after weighting for the population sizes) to 15.0. The majority of the suicide were males, and 60% were under the age of 29. Alcohol intoxication was common in the suicides, firearms the most popular method followed by hanging (while wrist slashing and gunshot were the most popular methods for attempting suicide), and sickness and the death of a loved one were common motivations.

Trott, et al. (1981) examined the 2656 deaths in Manitoba in 1976 investigated by the Medical Examiner (out of 8315 deaths). Drugs were involved in 36% of the deaths, primarily alcohol, alone or in combination with other drugs. These deaths included suicides, homicides and accidental deaths. In a multiple regression analysis, the involvement of drugs in the deaths was related to age (peaking for those aged 18 to 30), employment (higher in the unemployed) and ethnic status (higher in Canadian Indians and Eskimos) for both men and women. Although this study included deaths other than suicide, it does suggest that ethnic status is associated with drug-related deaths independently of employment and age.

Jarvis and Boldt (1982) examined all deaths among Canadian Indians in nine constituencies in Alberta in 1976. For the Canadian Indians, 11.7% of the male deaths and 8.6% of the female deaths were due to suicide compared to 3.3% and 1.7% for the total Alberta population. Seventy-two percent of the Canadian Indian suicides had alcohol detected in their blood, and 62% were judged to have chronic problems with alcohol abuse.

Garro (1988) examined suicidal behavior in Manitoba from 1973-1982, a province with a Canadian Indian population of around 43,000. The suicide rate for this group during the period was 40.1 per 100,000 per year, which contrasts with a suicide rate of 14.0 for Canada as a whole. The peak rate was for Canadian Indian males aged 15-29. Eighty-four percent of the Canadian Indian suicides were male, and 84% were between the ages of 10 and 39. Shooting was the most common method (55%) followed by hanging (26%).

Garro divided the province by the 53rd parallel; the northern communities are more remote, often inaccessible except by air in the winter, whereas the southern communities are more accessible. The suicide rate in the northern communities was 18.7 and in the southern communities 48.2. Looking at the suicide rate by tribe confirmed this difference: in the north, the Chipewyan had a suicide rate of 13 and the Ojibway [Northern] 5. The Cree in the middle of the province had a suicide rate of 22 and the Objibway (Salteaux) in the south had a rate of 48 and the Sioux 80. Garro examined the effect of the community banning alcohol; he found that easier access to alcohol in the northern communities was associated with a higher suicide rate but this was not true for the southern communities.

Ross and Davis (1986) studied a remote community of 3,448 people in Manitoba from 1981-1984. There were eight suicides, seven by men and six by hanging. The suicide rate for the treaty Indians was 83, for non-treaty Indians 52 and for non-Natives zero. Treaty Indians also had rates of attempted suicide (640 for men and 2003 for women, as compared to 80 and 226 respectively for non-treaty Indians).

Aldridge and St. John (1991) studied suicide in those aged 10 to 19 in Labrador from 1977-1988. The non-Canadian Indian suicide rate was 11.8. For Canadian Indian communities on the isolated northern coast, the suicide rate was 180, while for Canadian Indian communities elsewhere in the province it was zero. Overall, the suicide rate for Canadian Indian youths was 45

Fox, et al. (1984) studied a Manitoulin Island reserve whose suicide rate in 1971-1974 was 23.4 and in 1976-1980 27.7, but which experienced eight suicides in 1975 giving a suicide rate for that year of 267. The suicides were male, with a median age of 22, socially isolated, unskilled, alcohol abusers, and overly dependent upon their families for interpersonal support. Fox noted that, after 1975, the attempted suicide rate dropped on the reserve (from 11.7 in 1975 to 4.3 in 1981). (The average attempter was a female, median age 24, who used an overdose.)

We can conclude that the suicide rate among Canadian Indians is higher than that for the general population, and this increased suicide rate is more noticeable in the youth and in men. Interestingly, in Canada, the suicide rate of Canadian Indians is lower in rural areas than in urban areas, opposite to the difference reported for the USA.

Florida

Copeland (1989) reported a suicide rate for nonwhites in Dade County, Florida, for 1982-1986 of 5 per 100,000 per year: 11 for American Indians, 13.9 for black-Hispanics and 3.1 for Haitians. However, the rate for American Indians was based on only one suicide.

New Mexico

Becker, et al. (1990) reported on suicide rates in New Mexico by ethnic group from 1958-1987. Male American Indian suicide rates were higher throughout the period than those for non-Hispanic whites and Hispanics. For example, in 1983-1987, the suicide rate for male American Indians was 39.9, for non-Hispanic whites 30.8 and for Hispanics 25.9. The suicide rate for American Indians was especially high for males aged 15 to 34. Female American Indian suicide rates were, however, the lowest of the three ethnic groups throughout the period: 8.6 for non-Hispanic whites, 5.0 for Hispanics and 2.7 for American Indians.

Miller (1979) studied suicide on an anonymous reservation in the southwestern United States from 1968-1979. The suicide rate in 1977 was 57.8 compared with 21.5 for the state and 13.3 for the United States. The modal suicide occurred on the reservation, between 4 a.m. and 11 a.m., on Saturday or Sunday, in March/April or July/August, by firearm, and was male, single, employed as a laborer or a student, and with a median age of 20.

May and Van Winkle (1994) studied suicide in American Indians under the age of 30 in New Mexico from 1957-1987. Suicide rates were highest in the Apache, next highest in the Pueblo and lowest in the Navajo. The modal suicide was male, single and employed, used firearms most commonly, followed by hanging (with hanging gaining in popularity in the 1980's), who committed suicide at home, with alcohol abuse and alcohol intoxication at the time (with depression and mental illness becoming more common in the 1980's). The monthly peak has moved from May/November in the 1960's and 1970's to August/September in the 1980's, but the numbers were small here. Suicides seem to decline at the end of the month, and peak on Saturdays and Sundays and from 4 p.m. to midnight.

Pacific Northwest

Shore (1972) looked at suicidal behavior among the American Indians of the Pacific Northwest (Idaho, Oregon and Washington) in 1969, encompassing an American Indian population of some 40,000, of whom 24,000 lived on reservations. The West Coast group used to live in coastal villages and subsisted by fishing. The Plateau group lived by hunting in the past but today live by farming and lumbering. Both groups speak English fluently and have had close contact with whites.

In 1969, 75 individuals made 82 reported suicide attempts. The median age for both genders was 24, and 67% of the individuals were women. The most common marital status was single, followed by married. The average level of education was tenth grade (with no gender differences). The most common method was overdose, though the majority of the men used firearms or hanging. Attempts peaked from March to May, most took place at home, and the most common reasons were a quarrel with a relative or close friend and to express anger. Alcohol use was present in 56% of the incidents, and the most common diagnoses were adolescent adjustment reaction, alcohol addiction (more common in the men) and depressive reaction (more common in the women). There were five completed suicides during 1969, four men and one women, all living with parents, relatives or friends, and all single or separated. Two involved prisoners hanging themselves in jail. The suicide rate was 28 per 100,000 per year.

In a boarding school with 860 students (75% Alaskan Native, 21% Northwest Indian and 4% Navajo), there were 30 suicide attempts involving 24 students. The most common method was by overdose. The attempts clustered in early winter and spring, just before school holidays. (Though the suicidal students were not more likely to be drop-outs, incidents of dropping out followed the same temporal pattern.) The Northwest Indians were over-represented among these students, but only problem students from the Northwest Indian group were sent to this boarding school, whereas the other groups (Alaskan Natives and Navajo) were regular students.

Shore (1975) examined American Indian suicide rates in this region from 1969-1971. There were 20 completed suicides, 70% male, with a median age of 28 for men and 24 for women. Eighteen were single or separated, and eighteen were living with kin or friends. Fifty-five percent were intoxicated at the time of the suicide. The overall American Indian suicide rate in this sample was 28; the intermountain tribe had a rate of 122 while the northwest coastal tribes had a rate of 13 and plateau tribes 15. Thus, there was great tribal variation in suicide rates.

During the same period of time, there were 277 suicide attempts identified, 35% male, with a median age of 25 for both men and women. The intermountain tribes differed from the other northwest tribes in the pattern of attempted suicide. The intermountain tribe attempters were more often men, involved more alcohol and inhalant abuse, and occurred more often in jail.

Grossman, et al. (1994) examined the health status of Anglo and African Americans and American Indians in eight counties in Washington State from 1981-1990. The urban American Indians, like African Americans, were less educated than Anglo-Americans, and the rural American Indians were even less educated. The same differences were found for poverty and unemployment. For health factors related to births (low birth weight, teen-age mothers, etc.), the rural American Indians were better off than the urban American Indians and were more similar to the Anglo-Americans. Grossman, et al. reported suicide rates for these groups as follows: Anglo-Americans 14, African Americans 9, urban American Indians 17 and rural American Indians 26 (and the homicide rates were, respectively, 4, 30, 21 and 20).

Other

Stone (1992) looked at suicides examined by the medical examiner in Dallas County, Texas, and found that 0.5% of the 1200 cases involving firearms were American Indians which matched their percentage in the population of the county.

Suicide Clusters

Examples Of Suicide Clusters

Davidson (1989) reported on a cluster of thirteen suicides on the Wind River Reservation in Wyoming shared by the Northern Shoshoni and the Arapaho. Between January 1, 1985, and October 18, 1985, thirteen suicides occurred (12 Arapaho and one Shoshoni), whereas there were no suicides in 1983 and only one (a Shoshoni) in 1984. Twelve of the 13 were men, and all used hanging. Their ages ranged from 14 to 25. The calculated suicide rate for this period for men aged 15 to 24 was 1593 per 100,000 per year. Six of the suicides occurred off the reservation (two in jail and one at boarding school). All were buried on the reservation.[1]

---

[1] Coleman (1987) dates this same cluster as extending from August 12, 1985, to March 18, 1986, and says that there were ten suicides in the cluster, nine Arapaho and one Shoshoni. Long (1986) dates the cluster as occurring in 1985, with 12 completed suicides

Incidentally, Davis and Hardy (1986) derived a mathematical model for epidemics of suicide and found that their model predicted even more suicides in the Wind River cluster than actually occurred!

Ross and Davis (1986) noted two clusters of Canadian Indian suicide attempts in a remote small community in northern Manitoba, one precipitated by a fifteen year-old who attempted suicide and another with no obvious precipitant. A cluster of nine Eskimo [Yupik] suicides in an Alaska village has been described by Berendes (1988), and Kettl and Bixler (1991) noted five suicide in Alaska Natives in a 14 day period in 1983.

Coleman (1987) has also documented clusters of suicide among American Indians. In 1974, a seventeen-year old boy on a reservation in Northern Ontario, upset over the impending separation of his parents, drank some alcohol and shot himself in the head. Within a year, eight other youths committed suicide in the community of 37 families. The victims ranged in age from 17 to 31. Five of the nine were male, and all were single. Six used guns, and six committed suicide at or near their parents' home. Eight had been drinking, and all had low self-esteem. The rate of suicide for this community that year was 267. Ward and Fox (1977: Ward, et al., 1978) first described this cluster and noted that three victims had lost a parent, and two had severely ill parents. Only two of the victims had ever received psychiatric treatment, and only one suicide left a note. None were married or had any intimate relationships. They had low self-esteem and had been socially isolated since childhood. As a result, they were very dependent upon their families and, therefore, vulnerable to family discord. The victims coped with stress by escape, withdrawal, internalization and alcohol.

When is a Cluster a Cluster?

One problem with these studies is that there is rarely any attempt to show that the suicides occurring in a region really form a cluster or an epidemic. First, of course, these terms must be defined. But, having defined them,

---

and estimated the suicide rate for that year as 330 per 100,000 per year (though I calculate it to be 343). Long also noted 97 suicide attempts that year (though only 88 were verified).

there needs to be a sound methodological and statistical analysis to show that the suicides meet the criteria. Coleman noted that from 1949 to 1980, the Western Shoshoni and [Paiute] on the Duck Valley Indian Reservation in Nevada had 50 suicides, giving a suicide rate of 150, but a high rate of suicide is not the same as a cluster.

Fox, et al. (1984) found that in 1975 on a small Indian reserve in Canada, the suicide rate rose to 267 from a rate of about 25 before and after that year. Is this an epidemic or a cluster? In 1975, there were only eight suicides, and the suicide rate was high that year because the base population is small. Small populations will have greatly varying suicide rates from year to year because of their small size. In this community, each suicide contributes 33 to the annual suicide rate!

Bechtold (1988) reported a suicide cluster occurring in a "Plains Indian community," not further specified. The community was geographically remote, several hundred miles from the nearest city, with 80% unemployment, home to several tribes, with a total population of several thousand. In one eight-week period there were nine suicides, and four others in the same year (one before and three after the cluster). All were teenage or young adult males (13 to 28 years of age), all but one from the same tribe, and all used hanging. Alcohol use and abuse was prominent, as was an unstable home environment.

To illustrate that the "cluster" was indeed a cluster, Bechtold detailed the relationships among the suicides. For example, victim 2 died two weeks after victim 1 and had been a pall bearer at the funeral of victim 1. His girl friend was the first cousin of victim 3, and the girl friend of victim 3 was the sister of victim 1, etcetera.

Intervention and Prevention

Tower (1989) has provided a more detailed description of the Wind River Reservation cluster and the community's response to it. She noted that in August and September of 1985, there were 12 deaths from suicide and 88 verified suicide attempts or threats. For the completed suicides, four were 14 to 19 years of age and five were 23 to 26 years of age. Two of the suicides occurred in Indians in jail for intoxication. Of the 88 attempters, 52% were male, and alcohol was involved in 53% of the attempts. The greatest number of attempts were 13 to 19 years of age (45%), followed a group aged 20 to 29 (27%).

The community responded by providing crisis intervention and grief counseling through the Behavior Health Program on the reservation, the Community Health Representatives and the Community Mental Health Center. Several community meetings were held to provide information, and the Behavior Health Program worked with school counselors to identify students at risk and to carry out psychological autopsies on the suicides.

The Shoshoni and Arapaho tribes initiated a number of youth activities including extended hours for the school laboratories and gymnasiums, weekly alcohol-free teen dances, Halloween parties, field trips, etc. At the same time, the Indian Health Service and Bureau of Indian Affairs arranged for hospitalization of drunken Indians rather than jail. All adolescent suicide attempters were admitted for short-term psychiatric care. An Emergency Task Force of mental health and law enforcement personnel was formed, and a 24-hour emergency coverage was instituted.

In October, tribal spiritual leaders joined together for a traditional medicine ceremony which was held after the ninth suicide. After this, no further deaths occurred, though attempts continued to remain at a high level for a further two months.

Tower noted that the media coverage had made the situation much worse, and the tribal leaders eventually barred reporters from the reservation. The peak in attempts coincided with the peak in the media coverage of the epidemic. The Indian Health Service brought in outside consultants, but Tower states that their reception on the reservation was "mixed," implying that their presence was not helpful.

After the crisis, the community continued to work to improve the mental health of the community. A grant was obtained to prevent violence, suicide and alcoholism, and several programs established: parent groups, cultural/recreational groups, consumer action groups, etc. Business and employment opportunities were created, efforts were made to uncover and prevent child abuse and neglect, and improved treatment facilities were established for alcoholism. This was especially important since it was discovered that there was a high incidence of untreated depression in young males, who lacked job skills and abused alcohol, and who were involved in marital and child custody problems.

Efforts were made to prevent another epidemic of suicidal behavior on the anniversary of the first epidemic. The services provided during the initial epidemic were re-emphasized (such as grief counseling for the bereaved, community and parent meetings, and a ban on media coverage), but Tower felt that the traditional spiritual ceremonies performed during the anniversary were most helpful.

Tower stressed the need for communities to continue to act after the initial epidemic has abated. Rather than feeling relief that the crisis is over and returning to the old ways, communities need to hold debriefing meetings to discuss what has been learned, plan programs for the future to prevent similar epidemics, and seek funding for the proposals they develop.

SUICIDE IN CUSTODY

American Indians who commit crimes against tribal, local government or federal laws, on or off the reservation, can be placed in a variety of facilities operated by the tribes, the Bureau of Indian Affairs, and city, county, state or federal authorities. The Bureau of Indian Affairs and tribal facilities number about 72 and typically house the police, tribal court and jail. The majority of inmates in these jails are detained because of alcohol-related offenses. The profile of the typical jail suicide in America is a young male detained for minor offenses, often alcohol-related (Lester and Danto, 1993), and the typical American Indian inmate of reservation jails fits this profile.

Most of the jails are designed as maximum security facilities. Adequate supervision of the cells requires a greater number of staff than is typically available, and only intermittent patrol of the cell blocks takes place. At nights, often only the police dispatcher is available for supervising the inmates of the jail. In such situations, inmate suicidal behavior is likely to be more common. In many jurisdictions, American Indian youth are housed with adult prisoners, a practice that has been shown in America as a whole to increase the risk of youth suicide (Flaherty, 1973)

Duclos, et al. (1994) enumerated the various ways in which American Indian jails need to be improved: there are limited historical data with which to compare trends; the jails have rudimentary information systems even today (for example, they are typically not computerized); the various agencies are fragmented and often do not cooperate; the documentation about inmates is often inadequate and inaccurate (for example, it is for legal rather than management purposes); much suicidal behavior goes undocumented because of the tolerant attitude of the criminal justice personnel toward the inmates and because of the stigma which may be attached to suicide in the community, and this lack of documentation extends to the warning signs for suicidal behavior; suicide risk assessments are rarely conducted on new inmates; the detention staff lack training in mental health and suicide prevention; and the design of the facilities is often poor from the stand-point of suicide prevention.

All in all, detention facilities for American Indians fail most of the recommendations and standards proposed for preventing inmate suicidal behavior (Lester and Danto, 1993).

The Data

Grossman (1992) noted that in the Canadian federal prison for women (housing about 110 women, one quarter of whom were Canadian Indians), six Canadian Indian women committed suicide in two years. Grossman examined the two major theories about suicide in prison for their relevance for Indian women: deprivation theories (the prison itself causes the suicides) and importation theories (the prisoner has certain traits that make suicide more likely).

Relevant to deprivation theories, Grossman noted that the social isolation of prison, both from the home community and, if the inmate is placed in isolation in the prison, from the other prisoners, may be especially difficult for Indian women to cope with. There is racism and discrimination for the Indian women, both from the staff and other inmates. Even the helping services available are white-oriented culturally rather than Indian-oriented culturally. The Indian women lose control over their destiny, like other female inmates, but perhaps suffers more shame and social disgrace in the eyes of her home community.

Relevant to importation theories, Grossman noted that Indian women are the most disadvantaged group in Canada, worse off than Indian men. They have less education, more unemployment, earn less when employed (and those who cannot pay fines are more likely to be imprisoned), have a higher suicide rate in the community than white women in Canada, and have a history of physical and sexual abuse as children and as adults. Indeed, Grossman noted that the rate of Indian women murdering husbands has increased in recent years, while the same behavior in white women has not.

Duclos, et al. (1994) surveyed the four facilities for housing American Indian juveniles in America in 1989 and found 22 attempted suicides and one completed suicide in these facilities (whose capacity was 66 inmates). In a survey of 17 adult and adult-plus-juvenile facilities, one reported an adult completed suicide in the past year, and 81% reported at least one adult suicide attempt (average 1.6). Fifty-seven percent reported at least one juvenile suicide attempt (average 1.7).

Simpson, et al. (1983) studied the Hopi Indian Reservation for 1979-1980 and found 38 completed and attempted suicides, eleven of which occurred in jail in people arrested for intoxication. Nine of the eleven used hanging.[2]

Comment

Suicide rates in American and Canadian Indians do appear to higher than for the general populations of both nations, at least in recent years. The peak in suicide rates among male American Indian youth are noteworthy.

---

[2] Anson (1983) looked at inmate suicides in the states of America in 1979. He found that the incidence of suicide in the prisons was not associated with the percentage of inmates who were American Indians. This study would have made more sense, of course, if Anson had studied the American Indian suicide rate in the prison system of each state, but such data were not available to him.

This is especially so for Alaska Natives, particular the young and those in rural areas. Lester (1982) surveyed nations of the world for the distribution by age of suicide rates, and found that this pattern was rare in males. More recent data (Lester, 1994) confirms this, though many nations now have a secondary peak in suicide rates for those aged 15 to 24, including Canada and Finland. The extraordinarily high suicide rate among young males appears to be characteristic only of aboriginal groups, such as Australian aborigines and American Indians and some underdeveloped societies such as Truk and other South Pacific Islands (Hezel, 1984). Girard (1993) has noted a similar tendency for only the most underdeveloped nations to have a peak in male suicide rates among the youth.

It would be of great interest to explore this high rate of suicide in American Indian male youth further. Is it found in urbanized American Indian youth as well as those still living on the reservation? Is it found in all reservations or only on some? How has the suicide rate in American Indian male youth changed over the last ten years -- is the peak among youth getting larger or smaller, for example? Furthermore, some comparative studies comparing suicidal behavior in American Indian youths and, for example, Micronesian and Australian aboriginal youth might be informative -- are the stressors and risk factors for suicide similar or different in these diverse cultures?

Bachman (1992) noted that African Americans have the highest homicide rates in the USA, followed by American Indians, with whites having the lowest homicide rates. In contrast, African Americans have the lowest suicide rates with whites and American Indians much higher. Looking at the suicide/homicide rate ratio, the net result is that African Americans appear to be an outwardly aggressive group with suicide/homicide rate ratios of about 0.15 in the early 1980's; whites appear to be an inwardly aggressive group with ratios of about 0.74, and American Indians appear to be balanced in the direction of expression of aggression with ratios of about 0.56.

References

Aldridge, D., & St. John, K. Adolescent and pre-adolescent suicide in Newfoundland and Labrador. *Canadian Journal of Psychiatry*, 1991, 36, 432-436.

Anon. *Statistical profile on Native mental health.* Ottawa, Ontario: Medical Services Branch, 1990-1991.

Anson, R. H. Inmate ethnicity and the suicide connection. *Prison Journal*, 1983, 63(1), 91-99.

Bachman, R. *Death and violence on the reservation.* New York: Auburn House, 1992.

Balikci, A. *Suicidal behavior among the Netsilik Eskimos.* Ottawa, Ontario: Department of Northern Affairs and National Resources, 1960a. Publication number 60-2 of the Northern Co-ordination and Research Centre.

Balikci, A. Research patterns on Arvilikjuarmiut suicide patterns. *Review & Newsletter: Transcultural Research in Mental Health*, 1960b, #8(July), 35-36.

Bechtold, D. W. Cluster suicide in American Indian adolescents. *American Indian & Alaska Native Mental Health Research*, 1988, 1(3), 26-35.

Becker, T. M., Samet, J. M., Wiggins, C. L., & Key, C. R. Violent deaths in the West. *Suicide & Life-Threatening Behavior*, 1990, 20, 324-334.

Berendes, M. A tale told twice. In D. Lester (Ed.) *Suicide '88*. Denver, CO: American Association of Suicidology, 1988, 179-180.

Butler, G. C. Incidence of suicide among the ethnic groups of the Northwest Territories and Yukon Territory. *Medical Services Journal, Canada*, 1965, 22, 252-256.

Cooper, M., Corado, R., Karlberg, A. M., & Adams, L. P. Aboriginal suicide in British Columbia. *Canada's Mental Health*, 1992, 40(3), 19-23.

Coleman, L. *Suicide clusters*. Boston: Faber & Faber, 1987.

Copeland, A. R. Suicide among nonwhites. *American Journal of Forensic Medicine & Pathology*, 1989, 10, 10-13.

David, B. R., & Hardy, R. J. A suicide epidemic model. *Social Biology*, 1986, 33, 291-300.

Davidson, L. E. Suicide clusters and youth. In C. R. Pfeffer (Ed.) *Suicide among youth*. Washington, DC: American Psychiatric Press, 1989, 83-99.

Duclos, C. W., LeBeau, W., & Elias, G. L. American Indian adolescent suicidal behavior in detention environments. *American Indian & Alaska Native Mental Health Research*, 1994, 4, monograph, 189-221.

Flaherty, M. G. The national incidence of juvenile suicide in adult jails and juvenile detention centers. *Suicide & Life-Threatening Behavior*, 1983, 13, 85-94.

Forbes, N., & van der Hyde, V. Suicide in Alaska from 1978 to 1985. *American Indian & Alaska Native Mental Health Research*, 1988, 1(3), 36-55.

Fox, J., Manitowabi, D., & Ward, J. A. An Indian community with a high suicide rate. *Canadian Journal of Psychiatry*, 1984, 29, 425-427.

Garro, L. C. Suicides by status Indians in Manitoba. *Arctic Medical Research*, 1988, 47, supplement 1, 590-592.

Girard, C. Age, gender, and suicide. *American Sociological Review*, 1993, 58, 553-574.

Grossman, M. G. Two perspectives on aboriginal female suicides in custody. *Canadian Journal of Criminology*, 1992, 34, 403-416.

Grossman, D. C., Krieger, J. W., Sugarman, J. R., & Forquera, R. A. Health status of urban American Indians and Alaska Natives. *Journal of the American Medical Association*, 1994, 271, 845-850.

Havighurst, R. J. The extent and significance of suicide among American Indians today. *Mental Hygiene*, 1971, 55, 174-177.

Health Canada. *Suicide in Canada*. Ottawa: Health Canada, 1994.

Hezel, F. X. Cultural patterns in Trukese suicide. *Ethnology*, 1984, 23, 193-206.

Hislop. T., Threlfall, W., Gallagher, R., & Band, P. R. Accidental and intentional violent deaths among British Columbia native Indians. *Canadian Journal of Public Health*, 1987, 78, 271-274.

Hisnanick, J. J. Comparative analysis of violent deaths in American Indians and Alaska Natives. *Social Biology*, 1994, 41, 96-109.

Hlady, W. G., & Middaugh, J. P. The epidemiology of suicide in Alaska, 1983-1984. *Alaska Medicine*, 1987, 29, 158-164.

Hlady, W. G., & Middaugh, J. P. Suicides in Alaska. *American Journal of Public Health*, 1988, 78, 179-180.

Jacobs, J. *Adolescent suicide*. New York: Wiley, 1972.

Jarvis, G. K., & Boldt, M. Death styles among Canada's Indians. *Social Science & Medicine*, 1982, 16, 1345-1352.

Justice, J. W. Changing patterns of suicides in American Indians 1981 through 1983. Annual meeting, Northwest Indian Health Board, Portland, OR, 1985.

Kettl, P. A., & Bixler, E. O. Suicide in Alaska Natives 1979-1984. In D. Lester (Ed.) *Suicide '88*. Denver, CO: American Association of Suicidology, 1988a, 175-176.

Kettl, P. A., & Bixler, E. O. Season of birth and suicide. In D. Lester (Ed.) *Suicide '88*. Denver, CO: American Association of Suicidology, 1988b, 207-208.

Kettl, P. A., & Bixler, E. O. Suicide in Alaska Natives 1979-1984. *Psychiatry*, 1991, 54, 55-63.

Kost-Grant, B. L. Self-inflicted gunshot wounds among Alaska Natives. *Public Health Reports*, 1983, 98, 72-78.

Kramer, M., Pollack, E. S., Redick, R. W., & Locke, B. Z. *Mental disorders/suicide*. Cambridge, MA: Harvard University Press, 1972.

Kraus, R. F. Changing patterns of suicidal behavior in North Alaskan Eskimo. *Transcultural Psychiatric Research Review*, 1972, 9(April), 69-71.

Kraus, R. F. Suicidal behavior in Alaska Natives. *Alaska Medicine*, 1974, 16(1), 2-6.

Kraus, R. F., & Buffler, P. A. Intercultural variation in mortality due to violence. In E. F. Foulks, R. M. Wintrob, J. Westermeyer & A. R. Favazza (Eds.) *Current perspectives in cultural psychiatry.* New York: Spectrum, 1977, 81-91.

Kraus, R. F., & Buffler, P. A. Sociocultural stress and the American Native in Alaska. *Culture, Medicine & Psychiatry*, 1979, 3, 111-151.

Kraus, R. F., & Buffler, P. A. Suicide in Alaskan Natives. In R. J. Shephard & S. Itoh (Eds.) *Proceedings of the 3rd. International Symposium on Circumpolar Health.* Toronto, Ont.: University of Toronto, 1976, 556-557.

Lester, D. The distribution of sex and age among completed suicides. *International Journal of Social Psychiatry*, 1982, 28, 256-260.

Lester, D. Suicide in the elderly. In D. Lester & M. Tallmer (Eds.) *Now I lay me down.* Philadelphia: Charles Press, 1994, 1-16.

Lester, D., & Danto, B. L. *Suicide behind bars.* Philadelphia: Charles Press, 1993.

Long, K. A. Suicide intervention and prevention with an Indian adolescent population. *Issues in Mental Health Nursing*, 1986, 8, 247-253.

Mao, Y., Mologhney, B. W., & Semenciw, R. M. Indian reserve and registered Indian mortality in Canada. *Canadian Journal of Public Health*, 1992, 83, 350-353.

Mao, Y., Morrison, H., Semenciw, R., & Wigle, R. Mortality on Canadian Indian reserves 1977-1982. *Canadian Journal of Public Health*, 1986, 77, 263-268.

Maris, R. W. Suicide, status and mobility in Chicago. *Social Forces*, 1967, 46, 246-256.

May, P. A., & Dizmang, L. H. Suicide and the American Indian. *Psychiatric Annals*, 1974, 4(11), 22-28.

May, P. A.,, & Van Winkle, N. Indian adolescent suicide. *American Indian & Alaska Native Mental Health Research*, 1994, 4, monograph, 2-23.

McIntosh, J. L., & Santos, J. F. Suicide among minority elderly. *Suicide & Life-Threatening Behavior*, 1981, 11, 151-166.

Miller, M. Suicides on a southwestern Indian reservation. *White Cloud Journal*, 1979, 1(3), 14-18.

Ogden, M., Spector, M. I., & Hill, C. A. Suicides and homicides among Indians. *Public Health Reports*, 1970, 85, 75-80.

Parkin, M. Suicide and culture in Fairbanks. *Psychiatry*, 1974, 37, 60-67.

Prince, C. Recognition of predisposing factors which affect the high suicide rate of Canadian Indians. *Arctic Medical Research*, 1988, 47, supplement 1, 588-589.

Ross, C. A., & Davis, B. Suicide and parasuicide in a northern Canada Native community. *Canadian Journal of Psychiatry*, 1986, 31, 331-334.

Shore, J. H. Suicide and suicide attempts among American Indians of the Pacific Northwest. *International Journal of Social Psychiatry*, 1972, 18, 91-96.

Shore, J. H. American Indian suicide. *Psychiatry*, 1975, 38, 86-91.

Simpson, S. G., Reid, R., Baker, S. P., & Teret, S. Injuries among the Hopi Indians. *Journal of the American Medical Association*, 1983, 249, 1873-1876.

Stone, I. C. Characteristics of firearms and gunshot wounds as markers of suicide. *American Journal of Forensic Medicine & Pathology*, 1992, 13, 275-280.

Teicher, J. D. Suicide and suicide attempts. In J. B. Noshpitz (Ed.) *Basic handbook of child psychiatry, Volume 2: Disturbances of development*. New York: Basic Books, 1979, 685-697.

Tonkin, R. S. Suicide methods in British Columbian adolescents. *Journal of Adolescent Health Care*, 1984, 5, 172-177.

Tower, M. A suicide epidemic in an American Indian community. *American Indian & Alaska Native Mental Health Research*, 1989, 3(1), 34-44.

Trott, L., Barnes, G., & Dumoff, R. Ethnicity and other demographic characteristics as predictors of sudden drug-related deaths. *Journal of Studies on Alcohol*, 1981, 42, 564-578.

Ward, J. A., & Fox, J. A suicide epidemic on an Indian reserve. *Canadian Psychiatric Association Journal*, 1977, 22, 423-426

Ward, J. A., Fox, J., & Evans, A. L. Suicide epidemic among Canadian Indians. In V. Aalberg (ed.) *Proceedings of the 9th International Congress of the International Association for Suicide Prevention.* Helsinki, Finland: Finnish Association for Mental Health, 1978, 402-406.

Chapter 4

THE CAUSES OF SUICIDE IN AMERICAN INDIANS: PSYCHOLOGICAL FACTORS

There has been some research on the psychological causes of suicidal behavior in American Indians, and there has also been a good deal of speculation which has not been followed up with research to test the hypotheses generated by this speculation. In this chapter we will review both these ideas and the research which has been conducted.

PSYCHOLOGICAL SPECULATION

Depression

Jilek-Aall (1988) has suggested that American Indians suffer from *anomic depression*, a psychological state in which they feel useless and helpless in the face of rapid cultural change. Life on the reservation is often tedious, and there is little do except watch television and drink. The programs on television, however, show a standard of living far beyond that which they have, which frustrates them even more. Anomic depression has several components: (1) anomie, the absence of accepted norms combined with cultural identity confusion, and (2) a chronic dysphoric state, with lack of self-respect, purpose or hope for the future.

Like others, Jilek-Aall noted the frequent experience of bereavement, neglect and abuse among American Indians, and the breakdown and social disorganization of the culture. Young American Indians have come also to see suicide as heroic, as it was in some of the tribes in times past. They hope that, in their death, they may receive the attention and acceptance which they longed for in life and, when asked, American Indian teenagers often equate bravery with the courage to commit suicide.

Some American Indian tribes have begun to counteract this anomic depression by cultivating tribal ceremonies such as the Spirit Dance in the North Pacific Coast tribes, and by devising activities such as traditional dancing, sports, plays, arts and language to combat boredom. These activities also bring the young and the old together, thereby strengthening the social bonds for everyone.

Red Horse (1992) noted that the cultural history and individual life experiences of the American Indian may predispose them to a learned helplessness form of depression (Seligman, 1974) in which they have learned that there is nothing they can do to change their life situation.[3] Because of this, Red Horse suggested that it may be necessary for counselors of suicidal and depressed Indians to be more active than typically counselors. Like Rosenthal (1986) who discussed crisis intervention techniques based on a learned helplessness theory of depression, Red Horse urged counselors to accompany clients to the referrals made for them, rather than letting them go alone into these alienating situations, and to intervene personally in efforts to change the client's lives.

A Psychoanalytic Viewpoint

Hippler (1969), approaching the etiology of suicide from a psychoanalytic point of view, suggested that the causes for the patterns of suicide found in American Indians groups lay in their childhood rearing experiences. Suicide

[3] The high incidence of physical violence among American Indians, especially when intoxicated, suggests that the psychoanalytic form of depression (repressed and suppressed anger turned inward onto the self) may not be common among them.

can result from the desire to be reunited with the mother in a blissful state of fusion. As a result, suicidal individuals show strong dependency problems in childhood that were not adequately resolved and problems with the expression of aggression, especially when frustrated by adult situations that elicit memories of childhood frustrations. Suicide can express both anger felt toward the self and anger felt toward others. Hippler illustrated this with a few examples.

The Nahane (Kaska) child is nursed generously and has its physical needs taken care of, but it is swaddled and not permitted any freedom to develop its motor skills. It is discouraged from crawling and walking. There is little pressure to be toilet trained, but expressing anger is punished. However, when the next sibling is born, the child is shunted aside and, if a boy, must turn to his father and male peers for attention. The Kaska male tries to be self-reliant as a defense against feeling lonely and afraid. He avoids love relationships out of fear of rejection because his mother rejected him earlier in his life. He has sex mechanically and fantasizes the act as a way of aggressing against women.

In this setting, men frequently make suicide attempts in the presence of other males, who respond by thwarting the suicidal individual's self-destructive intent. This elicits attention and expressions of caring for the would-be suicide.

Several commentators have noted that the Iroquois appear to have an oral character and strong dependency needs. They have an intense concern with food, and the women seek revenge on their frustrating husbands by taking poison. After their deaths, their husbands are held responsible and must make restitution which, although the abused wife cannot experience, she can anticipate because of her knowledge of the cultural customs.

Apache child-rearing is non-nurturant and frequently brutal. The mothers are typically ambivalent about the coming child while pregnant and, though they nurture the baby after birth, ignore it when the next baby arrives. They sometimes give the older children away or simply abandon them. Apache parents deflect any anger felt by the older children by telling them to express it toward other objects -- for example, they are told to go and torture animals. The only outlet for aggression which is permitted is through drinking and its attendant self-destructiveness. Apaches when drunk frequently engage in brutal and often fatal fights, actions that they would never engage in when sober.

Although in these (and other) cases, Hippler tried to relate the pattern of self-destructive behavior and suicide to the childhood experiences of the culture, he relies solely on anecdote and does not attempt any systematic study of the relationship.

Personal Qualities

LaFromboise and Bigfoot (1988) noted several features of American Indian life which may be relevant to the high incidence of suicide in American Indian adolescents. With respect to First cultural values, they noted that many American Indians experience conflict when they try to internalize the values of the dominant American culture or try to practice traditional roles. For example, among the Pueblo (Hopi), adolescent males whose parents have married outside of the clan or village have a high risk for suicide. The tribe sees such marriages as unacceptable, though the dominant American culture does not. The offspring of these marriages, however, are deprived of their ceremonial heritage and kinship affiliation.

LaFromboise and Bigfoot noted that four values common to American Indians (self-control, independence, reciprocity and social responsibility) may be relevant to adolescent suicide among American Indians. The demand for self-control leads them to internalize pain rather than express it outwardly, and thus they are less likely to seek help or be seen by others to be in need of help. Adolescent American Indians also complain of being given too much independence and responsibility. They are expected by their families to make major decisions about their lives (such as about education) for which they are not equipped. Suicidal behavior often occurs when they feel overwhelmed and helpless in the face of these demands.

Reciprocity and social responsibility come into play during the funerals of suicides, at which time the deceased tend to be idealized, tempting others to join them. It is common for siblings to commit suicide on the anniversaries of their brothers' or sisters' suicidal deaths.

Among the cultural beliefs that may increase the risk of suicide is the prevalent belief in reincarnation among many American Indian tribes. Some tribes believe, for example, that the deceased are reborn into the same families or clans, and they make an effort to identify from whom the newborn baby derived its spirit. The reciprocity between the spirit world and the earthly world may reduce some of the fear concerning death, removing one of the inhibiting factors for suicide.

LaFromboise and Bigfoot also pointed to the ambiguity of identity in adolescent American Indians as a result of the conflict between the American Indian culture and the dominant American culture, and LaFromboise and Bigfoot suggested that this conflict may be greater for American Indian adolescents than for other ethnic groups, especially because the other ethnic groups have lives more intertwined with the dominant culture. Even urban ghettos are more integrated into the dominant culture than reservations. LaFromboise and Bigfoot suggested that American Indians adolescents adopted by white families may feel this conflict in a particularly severe form, though they do not say why this might be so as compared to other non-white and non-American children adopted from abroad by many white American families.

LaFromboise and Bigfoot also noted the high incidence of loss in American Indian youth, especially from deaths of and separations from relatives. American Indian youths are very likely to have been cared for by more than one significant other, by caretakers who have been arrested, and by parents who have deserted the family or who have been divorced. The adolescents themselves are also likely to have been arrested at a young age and sent to boarding schools.

These losses and separations, combined with the everyday hardship of living (arising from long-term poverty, social and political tension, unemployment, and underachievement in education) serve to undermine the adolescent's self-esteem and coping efforts.

As a result of this analysis, LaFromboise and Bigfoot established a counseling program for American Indian adolescents which dealt with some of these problems. For example, the program educated the adolescents about self-control coping strategies, teaching them the kinds of statements to say to themselves when overwhelmed ("My cousin refused to be beaten down or quit," "I want a better life for my children," or "Hassles are a part of life; it will get better"). The adolescents were also educated about the coping resources within their communities, and they were trained in problem-solving techniques. It can be seen from the work of LaFromboise and Bigfoot that having a hypothesis about the causes of suicidal preoccupation in the target group can suggest particular counseling strategies which might be particularly useful for the group.

Other Suggestions

Berlin (1986) suggested that suicidal behavior in American Indian adolescents was made more likely by the use of alcohol by their mothers when they were pregnant with the babies and by alcoholism and depression in the mothers which interferes with effective parenting. The children, as they grow up, show the effects of this early poor parenting by abusing inhalants, alcohol and drugs such as marijuana and hallucinogens, by becoming depressed, and by getting pregnant as while still teenagers.

Incidentally, Berlin noted that many of the parents of today's suicidal adolescents had been placed in boarding schools when they were young and, if they were active in the community, were often the militants in the move toward the restoration of traditional values.

Are Standard Psychological Tests Reliable and Valid for American Indians?

Before looking at the research which has been conducted on American Indians, we must address an important issue -- whether the psychological tests used for research on American Indians, which were devised for whites, are reliable or valid for American Indians. Many of the commentators who mention this issue produce no evidence that the tests lack reliability and validity for American Indians, but a few studies have been published which address this issue.

Dick, et al. (1992) gave the Reynolds (1988) Suicide Ideation Questionnaire to American Indian high school students. The mean score of the group was similar to that of the standardization sample. The internal consistency reliability (calculated with Cronbach's alpha) was very high (0.96 for the overall scale). Item-total correlations were similar to those for the standardization sample. Thus, the reliability of the test for American Indians was excellent.

As part of the validity studies, Dick found that scale scores were positively associated with depression scale scores (Pearson $r = 0.67$) and anxiety scale scores ($r = 0.65$) as expected. Thus, the scale appears to have construct validity for this group. (Incidentally, the scales used to measure depression and anxiety also had good reliability for this group of subjects.)

Enriquez (1971) gave a suicide inventory to English-speaking Navajo youth in both an English and a Navajo version (in counterbalanced order for two subgroups of the sample). The scores obtained on the nine subscales were virtually identical in the two versions. However, the correlations between scores on the suicide preoccupation scale and the other subscale scores differed slightly for the two versions. In the English version, suicidal preoccupation was associated with depression, immaturity, anxiety, anomie, aggression, social prejudice and dependency but not with rigidity. In the Navajo version, suicidal preoccupation was associated only with depression, immaturity, anxiety, and aggression.

It may be concluded that there is no sound evidence to indicate that the standard psychological tests used by psychologists to study mainly white populations cannot be appropriately used with American Indians who speak English fluently.

INDIAN VERSUS NON-INDIAN SUICIDES

Cooper, et al. (1992) compared Canadian Indian suicides in British Columbia with suicides in other ethnic groups. They found many differences. The Canadian Indian suicides were more likely to have grown up in families with alcohol abuse, suicidal behavior and childhood sexual and physical abuse.

The Canadian Indian suicides were more often alcohol or drug abusers, more often had a history of physical or verbal violence as victim or abuser, were less often diagnosed as having a psychiatric disorder and less often had received psychiatric treatment. The two groups did not differ in recent stressful life events. More of the Canadian Indians were intoxicated at the time of the suicide, and slightly fewer gave warning signs of the suicide (two-thirds versus four-fifths). Fewer of the Canadian Indians had consulted a health professional in the preceding year, but slightly more of the Canadian Indians had attempted suicide in the past.

The Canadian Indian suicides peaked in October to December, on Saturday/Sunday, and from midnight to 6 a.m. Although Cooper did not give the corresponding data for the other suicides, this distribution is unusual. Most of the Canadian Indians committed suicide in their own home, and just under a half of the suicidal actions were planned, with only 15% being spur-of-the-moment actions. One third used firearms and another third hanging. Cooper noted that the non-Canadian Indian suicides showed no temporal distribution, were less impulsive, used firearms more often and committed suicide more often at home while not intoxicated.

Elliott, et al. (1990) compared high school Canadian Indian students from a reserve in Manitoba with white rural Canadian youths. Twice as many Canadian Indians had attempted suicide (27% versus 12%), though this difference was not statistically significant, and three times as many met the criteria for a diagnosis of depression. However, differences in hopelessness and current suicidal ideation were not statistically significant.

Among the Canadian Indians, the attempters were older and were more likely to have current suicidal ideation than the non-attempters, and the depressed Canadian Indians had experienced more recent stressors and had higher hopelessness scores, though not more current suicidal ideation, than the nondepressed youths. Canadian Indians who were currently suicidal were more likely to have known a suicidal individual and had been suicidal more often in the past than the nonsuicidal youths.

Among the whites, those with depression had higher hopelessness scores and more current suicidal ideation than the nonsuicidal youths. Those who had attempted suicide had more recent stressors and were more likely to have current suicidal ideation than the non-attempters. Those who had current suicidal ideation were more depressed, had experienced more recent stressors, had attempted suicide more in the past and were more likely to have thought about suicide in the past than the nonsuicidal youths.

On the whole these results appear to be similar for Canadian Indians and whites -- depression, hopelessness and stress predict suicidal preoccupation.

STUDIES ON AMERICAN INDIAN SUICIDES

Travis (1983) identified 119 incidents of suicidal behavior in Kotzebue, an Alaskan village on the northwest coast of Alaska. All but three incidents were by Eskimos, and 16 were repeated incidents. Eight percent were completed suicides, 15% judged to be unsuccessful suicides, 58% attempted suicides and 19% suicidal gestures. The group was 57% female, and the average age was 22.5 years.

Comparing the suicidal men and women, the men were more educated, more often single, less often with no occupation, and more often used firearms for their suicide. The men and women did not differ in age, unemployment, acculturation (the number of months lived outside of the region), income, alcohol abuse, or place of residence.

Comparing the completed suicides/unsuccessful suicides with the attempters/gestures, Travis found that the completers/unsuccessful suicides were more often male, more educated, more acculturated, less often resided in Kotzebue, and more often used firearms for their suicide. Education proved to be the strongest factor here, after controls for age, gender and acculturation.

Shields (1979) compared the Rorschach ink-blot test responses of Alaskan Eskimos who had attempted suicide with normal Eskimos (a poor choice of a comparison group -- a depressed nonsuicidal comparison group would have been methodologically sound). He found that the suicidal Eskimos performed worse on three of the five measures he used: they performed worse on reality testing, drive and impulse control and synthesizing (or integrating) functions, but no differently on object relations and defense functioning.

Predicting Adolescent Suicidal Preoccupation

Sack, et al. (1994) surveyed American Indian and non-American Indian children in grades 2 and 4 and included the statement "I think about killing myself." Twenty-one percent of the Indian children and 20% of the non-Indian children agreed with this. (Sack, et al. claimed that this difference was statistically significant, but clearly it is not. Thus, there may be errors in their data presentation.) To the question "Do you think life is not worth living?" 21% of the Indian children and zero percent of the non-Indian children agreed.

Manson, et al. (1989) surveyed 179 American Indian adolescents (aged 12-20) at a boarding school in the southeastern United States. Twenty-three percent had previously attempted suicide; 20.9 percent had thought about suicide in the past month, 9.6 percent would have like to kill themselves, and 2.8 percent would have killed themselves had they been able to.

In a poorly carried out study, Harvey, et al. (1976) looked at the students in an Alaskan Native secondary boarding school whose students were 68% Eskimo. They noted that the students from small villages were often anxious and depressed, and some of these attempted suicide. Some students came from larger cities, but these students were at the school because their home schools had found them to be problems. These students often drank and acted-out when intoxicated. Not only is this study poor because the two groups of students are quite different and not comparable (all of the students from rural communities, but only problem children from urban communities), but it is hard to understand the rationale behind a social policy which mixes problem children from urban communities which have their own school districts with the regular students from rural communities. Harvey (1976) noted that suicidal gestures among the girls at this school were more common than expected in the Eskimo girls and less common than expected in the [Athabascan] and Southeast Indian girls. A history of attempted suicide and current suicidal ideation was not related to age, gender or the number of recent stressful life events, but these suicidal behaviors were associated with having relatives and friends who had completed and attempted suicide. While the death of a sibling or parent was not related to suicidal behavior, death of a friend was related (and almost half of these deaths were from suicide). Depression scores were related to prior and current suicidal behavior, while excessive alcohol use was associated with only prior suicide attempts. Perceived family support was associated with a history of suicide attempts while support from friends was associated with current suicidal ideation.

Dinges and Quang (1992-1993) studied 124 adolescents at a boarding school who had a depressive disorder, some of whom had attempted or considered suicide. They examined which stressful life events predicted suicidal behavior in these adolescents, and the most consistent predictor was parent/family conflict.

Dinges and Quang (1994) found that 41% of American Indian adolescents in a boarding school had seriously considered suicide, while 30% had attempted suicide. Gender and age were not related to these behaviors. A history of suicidal ideation was predicted by depression scores, alcohol and drug use, somatic symptoms, lower family cohesion and gender. A history of attempted suicide was predicted by depression scores, alcohol and drug use, somatic symptoms and less support from fathers.

Grossman, et al. (1991) administered a survey to 7,254 adolescents in grades 6 through 12 on the Navajo reservation. Fifteen percent admitted to a prior suicide attempt, and 58% of these had made more than one attempt. Only 15% of the attempts were brought to the attention of the medical services. The correlates of prior suicidal attempts were a history of mental health problems, feeling alienated from friends and community, having a friend who had attempted suicide, weekly consumption of hard liquor, a family history of suicidal behavior, a history of physical or sexual abuse, being female and perceiving one's health as poor. These correlates parallel those found for the general population (Lester, 1992a).

Gartrell, et al. (1993) surveyed 229 Canadian Indian school children aged 12 to 16 in central Alberta, all Cree (personal communication, John

Gartrell, June 9, 1995). About 15% had attempted suicide in the past. A history of suicidal ideation was more common in the older children, in females, if the father was absent from the home, if they smoked cigarettes and used alcohol or marijuana, if they were worried and felt bad, and if other family members had been suicidal. A history of attempting suicide was more common in the older children, in those worried and feeling bad, in those who smoked, used alcohol and marijuana, and when other family members had been suicidal.

Howard-Pitney, et al. (1992) surveyed 83 freshman high school children who were Pueblos (Zuni). Thirty percent reported a previous suicide attempt. (LaFromboise and Howard-Pitney [1994] noted that Zuni believe that imagining a suicide attempt can be construed as having acted upon that attempt, and they modified the questions exploring this is their subsequent research.) Suicidal ideation in these students was associated with the use of marijuana and drugs, depression, hopelessness, stress and psychological distress, self-perception of receiving poor social support, poor interpersonal communication abilities and parental drug and alcohol use. A history of suicide attempts was associated with being female, using alcohol, marijuana and drugs, suicidal ideation, depression, hopelessness, stress, psychological distress, making fewer efforts at coping, poor interpersonal communication abilities and not liking school.

LaFromboise and Howard-Pitney (1995) tested 84 female students from a Zuni high school in New Mexico (all Zuni) and 92 from a high school in Oklahoma comprising 56% Cherokee, 23% Creek, 9% Seminole and 1% Zuni. Thirty percent of the Oklahoma sample and 21% of the Zuni sample had attempted suicide in the past, though the Zuni attempters had attempted more often and more recently than the Oklahoma attempters.

Attempting suicide in the Oklahoma sample was associated with alcohol use but not with depression, hopelessness, liking for school, family dysfunction, social support or self-efficacy. Current suicide risk, however, was associated with all of the predictor variables. In the multiple regression analyses, only alcohol use predicted prior attempted suicide, while hopelessness and family dysfunction predicted suicide risk.

Attempting suicide in the Zuni sample was associated with depression, liking for school, alcohol use, social support and self-efficacy, while current suicide risk was associated with hopelessness, alcohol use, social support and self-efficacy. In the multiple regression analyses, attempting suicide in the past was predicted by depression, alcohol use and social support, while current suicidal risk was predicted by hopelessness and alcohol use.

Comment

Berlin (1987) noted that adolescent suicides among American Indians are characterized by loss of caretakers by death or divorce and a long arrest record in both the adolescent and the caretakers. The chaotic home environment which the youths appear to have experienced was seen by Berlin as similar to the pattern described for black and adolescent suicidal youths (Teicher, 1979) and, we might add, youths in general (Jacobs, 1972). Thus, the psychological and experiential factors increasing the risk of adolescent suicide appear to be the same for American Indians as other youths, but these factcrs may be more prevalent in the American Indian communities.

Koverola (1994) noted that Canadian Indian suicides typically come from families with family violence, inadequate parenting and neglect, chronic and widespread substance abuse and poverty, and she drew particular attention to physical and sexual abuse which she believed to be of particular relevance to suicide in these communities and which has been shown to be associated with an increased risk of subsequent suicidal behavior (Lester, 1992a). However, she provided no data to document the prevalence of sexual abuse of Canadian Indian children. Elliott (1992) has also stressed the widespread prevalence of childhood sexual and physical abuse in Canadian Indian communities as relevant to their suicidal behavior.

Predicting Adult Suicidal Preoccupation

Peniston (1978) gave the Minnesota Multiphasic Personality Inventory (MMPI) to thirty Ute Indians who had attempted suicide. Scores on the Depression scale of the MMPI were not significantly associated with the number of suicide attempts they had made, nor the number of attempts for which they were intoxicated. However Ego Strength scores were positively associated with the total number of suicide attempts, though not with the number of attempts for which they were intoxicated.

Westermeyer and Peake (1983) followed-up 45 alcoholic American Indians treated at a hospital in Minnesota for ten-years and found that nine had died (2% per year, a rather high rate compared to white alcoholics). One of the deaths was from suicide, two from murder and two in vehicular accidents, and all of the five were intoxicated at the time of death.

Zitzow and Desjarlait (1994) studied a sample of attempted suicides on an Ojibway reservation. The modal attempter was female, 15 to 19 years old, using pills, with less than one hour premeditation, uncertain about whether they wanted to die, with family problems as a stressor, and attempting from 6 p.m. to midnight on Saturdays.

Compared to the adolescent attempters, the adult attempters were more often from the traditional village on the reservation (in fact, members of this village were overrepresented among the attempters), more often male, more often attempting from 6 p.m. to 6 a.m., more often intoxicated with alcohol and drugs, with more prior suicide attempts, more often telling no-one about their attempt, more often wishing to die, making more lethal attempts, more often with partner problems, more often chronic alcohol/drug abusers but less often marijuana users), less often motivated by a wish to escape, less impulsive, and more often mentally confused than the adolescent attempters.

Comparing the men and women, the women were more likely to be living at home with their family, attempted more often from 2 p.m. to midnight, used pills more, less often abused alcohol, more often used marijuana, more often were victims of violence, and made fewer precautions against being discovered than the men.

A comparison of eight highly lethal attempters with four completed suicides indicated a great similarity, and so Zitzow and Desjarlait concluded that a continuum of suicidal intent exists, ranging from gestures through to completed suicide, much as Lester, et al. (1975, 1979) have argued.

Zitzow and Desjarlait devised a ten-item measure of suicidal intent based upon the circumstances of the suicide attempt, similar to the suicidal intent scale devised by Lester, et al. (1975, 1979), and identified four clusters of items which they labeled ruminating planners, wanting to die, confused reactives and manipulating ambivalents.

SPECIFIC PRECIPITANTS

Psychiatric Disorder

One important determinant of suicidal behavior in American Indians could be the particular type of psychiatric disorders which they are prone to develop. This has not been studied extensively, but some research suggests that there may be differences. For example, Jilek-Aall, et al. (1978) compared psychiatric patients they saw at their clinic in British Columbia, Canada, from three ethnic groups -- Coast Salish, Russian Doukhobors and Germanic Mennonites. Suicide attempts were more common among the patients from the Coast Salish than among patients from the other two ethnic groups, although suicidal preoccupation was equally common among the Coast Salish and the Mennonites. However, the three ethnic groups differed psychiatrically; the Coast Salish had more reactive-neurotic depression, the Doukhobors schizophrenia and the Mennonites affective psychosis. The Coast Salish had more alcohol and drug abuse, identity confusion, prolonged mourning reactions and hallucinations involving supernatural spirits, but fewer paranoid delusions, guilt, anxiety, sexual dysfunction and hypochondriasis. More extensive research into the particular psychiatric symptoms common in different American Indian tribes would be of great interest.

Alcohol Abuse

Alcohol abuse is strongly linked to suicidal behavior (Lester, 1992b). Alcohol abusers have a high incidence of suicide, and suicidal individuals have a high incidence of alcohol abuse. This association may be because alcohol abuse increases the severity of depression, which in turn increases the risk of suicide. The association may also result from the fact that alcohol abuse worsens the individual's life situation, thereby increasing the stressors to which the potentially suicidal person is subjected.

Alcohol abuse is common in American Indians. Kettl and Bixler (1993) matched 33 Alaska Natives who had committed suicide and who had received care at the Alaska Native Medical Center in Anchorage, with 33 controls matched for age and gender whose records followed the suicides in the files. The two groups did not differ in the incidence of psychiatric disorder (or type), psychiatric admissions or medical illness history. However, the suicides were more often alcohol abusers and more likely to have a history of prior suicide attempts. Kettl and Bixler noted how the suicide rate among Alaska Natives had risen from 13 per 100,000 per year in 1961-1965 to 67.6 in 1986. It would of interest to explore whether this increase is paralleled by an increase in alcohol abuse.

O'Nell (1993) interviewed 20 Flathead (Salish) and Kalispel (Pend d'Oreille) Indians on the Flathead Reservation in Montana. They were a non-random sample of depressed people, ten men and ten women, aged from 29 to 79. Twelve of the 20 had suffered from a major depressive disorder at some point in their lives, and four of these were diagnosed as having this disorder at the present time. Thirteen others were diagnosed as having a dysthymic disorder at the present time. Three of these dysthymic disorder individuals had a comorbid diagnosis other than alcohol abuse.

All twenty had experienced problem drinking behavior at some point in their lives. At least seven had been treated for alcohol abuse, and only six were currently sober. One had been a mild abuser, ten moderate and six severe. (It was considered inappropriate to interview three elders about their alcohol abuse.) With regard to lifetime comorbidity with alcohol abuse, all twelve individuals with a lifetime experience of a major depressive disorder had also been alcohol abusers. Of these twelve, six had the two problems at the same time. Eight of the people had attempted suicide; all had abused alcohol, and four had experienced a major depressive disorder at some time during their lives. Five of the 12 people with a major depressive disorder had attempted suicide, and all four of those with a major depressive disorder and alcohol abuse had attempted suicide.

O'Nell noted that depression was often seen as a positive expression in this community since it implied that the person was aware of the sadness of life. To be depressed was to be mature -- a carefree attitude was seen as immature. Drinking was seen as a positive expression of sociality, and refusing to drink was sometimes seen as a slight against family and friends, despite the fact that drunken people sometimes acted improperly.

Depression in this group had three components. Feeling grief-stricken was found in the older people who have suffered loss, and suicidal behavior was rare in these individuals since it would hurt those left behind and it would also transgress against the cultural norms. Feeling worthless, often found in the young men, was accompanied by feelings of guilt for being selfish, and did trigger suicidal behavior. Feeling aggrieved and angry at undeserved shame was not associated with major depressive disorders, but did trigger suicidal behavior in teenagers and jilted lovers. O'Nell suggested that feeling worthless in those who have both a major depressive disorder and who abuse alcohol is an indicator of serious suicidal inclinations.

The Child Welfare System

Bagley (1985) presented the case of suicide in a thirteen year-old Canadian Indian boy, providing extracts from his personal diary. The boy, Richard, was taken from a poor family and labeled as "neglected." Bagley noted that the system could easily have provided income and housing support to prevent his removal from his biological parents. They chose instead to place Richard in a series of foster homes where he was separated from his siblings and frequently abused. Richard was also mistreated by the social workers who gave no regard to his own needs, wishes or interests.

Bagley considered Richard's treatment to be abuse by the system. Had his parents been richer and had they lived in a more litigious society, the system could (and should) have been sued for damages. Such law suits often provoke reform. American and Canadian Indians have protested against the adoption of their children by white groups, but foster and adoptive parents are not necessarily abusive and capricious. In Richard's case, it is not that his foster parents and social workers were white that was at fault; rather it was that the foster parents were abusive and the system capricious.

Despite the powerful emotions aroused by Richard's case in Bagley's paper, research on the issues raised by the case is needed.

CONCLUSIONS

What has this research taught us about the psychological causes of American Indian suicide? Surprisingly, it appears that the predictors of suicidal behavior in American Indians are exactly the same as those for white suicide (see Lester, 1992a): depression, hopelessness, immaturity, aggressiveness, a history of suicidal behavior, psychiatric problems and substance abuse, parent and family conflict, lack of family support, physical and sexual abuse, and recent stress.

This complete parallel with the research on white suicide may mean one of two things. First, it may mean that the causes of suicide in American Indians are no different than those found for other ethnic groups, and this is quite likely. On the other hand, it may be that researchers have sought to use only those predictors identified from research on other ethnic groups and have not looked for what other psychological variables might contribute to the prediction of American Indian suicide. However, it would be difficult to suggest at the present time what these variables might be, and so perhaps we need more speculation of the kind we reviewed at the beginning of this chapter which might indicate to us what these new variables could be.

REFERENCES

Bagley, C. Child abuse by the child welfare system. *Journal of Child Care*, 1985, 2(3), 12-19.

Berlin, I. N. Psychopathology and its antecedents among American Indian adolescents. *Advances in Clinical Child Psychiatry*, 1986, 9, 125-152.

Berlin, I. N. Suicide among American Indian adolescents. *Suicide & Life-Threatening Behavior*, 1987, 17, 218-232.

Cooper, M., Corrado, R., Karlberg, A. M., & Adams, L. P. Aboriginal suicide in British Columbia. *Canada's Mental Health*, 1992, 40(3), 19-23.

Dick, R. W., Beals, J., Manson, S. M., & Bechtold, D. W. Psychometric properties of the Suicidal Ideation Questionnaire in American Indian adolescents. In D. Lester (ed.) *Suicide '92*. Denver, CO: American Association of Suicidology, 1992, 103-108.

Dinges, N. G., & Quang, D. T. Stressful life events and co-occurring depression, substance abuse and suicidality among American Indian and Alaska Native adolescents. *Culture, Medicine & Psychiatry*, 1992-1993, 16, 487-502.

Dinges, N. G., & Quang, D. T. Suicide ideation and suicide attempt among American Indian and Alaska Native boarding school adolescents. *American Indian & Alaska Native Mental Health Research*, 1994, 4, monograph, 167-188.

Elliott, C. A. Sexually and physically abused native youth. In D. Lester (Ed.) *Suicide '92*. Denver, CO: American Association of Suicidology, 1992, 61-62.

Elliott, C. A., Kral, M. J., & Wilson, K. G. Suicidal concerns among native youth. In D. Lester (Ed.) *Suicide '90*. Denver, CO: American Association of Suicidology, 1990, 283-285.

Enriquez, V. G. Navajo suicide. *Philippine Journal of Psychology*, 1971, 4(1), 70-73.

Gartrell, J. W., Jarvis, G. K., & Derksen, L. Suicidality among adolescent Alberta Indians. *Suicide & Life-Threatening Behavior*, 1993, 23, 366-373.

Grossman, D. C., Milligan, B. C., & Deyo, R. A. Risk factors for suicide attempts among Navajo adolescents. *American Journal of Public Health*, 1991, 81, 870-874.

Harvey, E. B. Psychiatric consultation and social work at a secondary school for Eskimo, Indian and Aleut students in Alaska. In R. J.

Shephard & S. Itoh (Eds.) *Circumpolar health.* Toronto: University of Toronto, 1976, 517-525.

Harvey, E. B., Gazay, L., & Samuels, B. Utilization of a psychiatric-social-work team in an Alaskan Native secondary boarding school. *Journal of the American Academy of Child Psychiatry*, 1976, 15, 558-574.

Hippler, A. E. Fusion and frustration. *American Anthropologist*, 1969, 71, 1074-1087.

Howard-Pitney, B., LaFromboise, T. D., Basil, M., September, B., & Johnson, M. Psychological and social indicators of suicidal ideation and suicide attempts in Zuni adolescents. *Journal of Consulting & Clinical Psychology*, 1992, 60, 473-476.

Jacobs, J. *Adolescent suicide.* New York: Wiley, 1972.

Jilek-Aall, L. Juvenile alcohol use and self-destructive behaviour in northern populations. *Arctic Medical Research*, 1988, 47, supplement 1, 604-610.

Jilek-Aall, L., Jilek, W., & Flynn, F. Sex role, culture and psychopathology. *Journal of Psychological Anthropology*, 1978, 1, 473-488.

Kettl, P. A., & Bixler, E. O. Alcohol and suicide in Alaska natives. *American Indian & Alaska Native Mental Health Research*, 1993, 5(2), 34-45.

Koverola, C. Sexual abuse as a precipitant of suicide in Native youth. *AAS Newslink*, 1994, 20(2), 9-10.

LaFromboise, T. D., & Bigfoot, D. S. Cultural and cognitive considerations in the prevention of American Indian adolescent suicide. *Journal of Adolescence*, 1988, 11, 135-153.

LaFromboise, T. D., & Howard-Pitney, B. The Zuni life skills development curriculum. *American Indian & Alaska Native Mental Health Research*, 1994, 4, monograph, 98-121.

LaFromboise, T. D., & Howard-Pitney, B. Suicidal behavior in American Indian female adolescents. In S. S. Canetto & D. Lester (Eds.) *Women and suicidal behavior.* New York: Springer, 1995, 157-173.

Lester, D. *Why people kill themselves*. Springfield, IL: Charles Thomas, 1992a.

Lester, D. Alcoholism and drug abuse. In R. W. Maris, A. L. Berman, J. T. Maltsberger & R. I. Yufit (Eds.) *Assessment and prediction of suicide*. New York: Guilford, 1992b, 321-336.

Lester, D., Beck, A. T., & Trexler, L. Extrapolation from attempted suicides to completed suicides. *Journal of Abnormal Psychology*, 1975, 84, 563-566.

Lester, D., Beck, A. T., & Mitchell, B. Extrapolation from attempted suicides to completed suicides. *Journal of Abnormal Psychology*, 1979, 88, 78-80.

Manson, S. M., Beals, J., Dick, R. W., & Duclos, C. Risk factors for suicide among Indian adolescents at a boarding school. *Public Health Reports*, 1989, 104, 609-614.

O'Nell, T. D. "Feeling worthless." *Culture, Medicine & Psychiatry*, 1993, 16, 447-469.

Peniston, E. G. The Ego Strength scale as a predictor of Ute Indian suicide risk. *White Cloud Journal*, 1978, 1(2), 15-18.

Red Horse, J. G. Treatment and prevention of suicide among American Indians. In E. W. Haller & L. P. Aitken (Eds.) *Mashkiki: Old medicine nourishing the new*. Lanham, MD: University Press of America, 1992, 69-79.

Reynolds, W. M. *Suicidal Ideation Questionnaire*. Odessa, FL: Psychological Assessment Resources, 1988.

Rosenthal, H. The learned helplessness syndrome. *Emotional First Aid*, 1986, 3(2), 5-8.

Sack, W. H., Beiser, M., Baker-Brown, G., & Redshirt, R. Depressive and suicidal symptoms in Indian school children. *American Indian & Alaska Native Mental Health Research*, 1994, 4, monograph, 81-96.

Seligman, M. Depression and learned helplessness. In R. J. Friedman & M. M. Katz (Eds.) *The psychology of depression*. New York: Wiley, 1974, 85-113.

Shields, J. R. Attempted suicide in Alaskan Eskimos. *Dissertation Abstracts International*, 1979, 39B, 5588-5589.

Teicher, J. D. Suicide and suicide attempts. In J. B. Noshpitz (Ed.) *Basic handbook of child psychiatry, Volume 2: Disturbances of development*. New York: Basic Books, 1979, 685-697.

Travis, R. Suicide in northwest Alaska. *White Cloud Journal*, 1983, 3(1), 23-30.

Westermeyer, J., & Peake, E. A ten-year follow-up of alcoholic Native Americans in Minnesota. *American Journal of Psychiatry*, 1983, 140, 189-194.

Zitzow, D., & Desjarlait, F. A study of suicide attempts comparing adolescents to adults on a Northern Plains American Indian reservation. *American Indian & Alaska Native Mental Health Research*, 1994, 4, monograph, 35-69.

Chapter 5

THE CAUSES OF SUICIDE IN AMERICAN INDIANS: SOCIOLOGICAL FACTORS

May and Dizmang (1974) noted that there were three major sociological theories which have been proposed for explaining the American Indian suicide rate. One theory focuses on *social disorganization*. The dominance of the Anglo-American culture has forced American Indian culture to change and has eroded traditional cultural systems and values. This changes the level of social regulationand social integration, important causal factors for suicide in Durkheim's (1897) theory of suicide.

A second theory focuses on *cultural conflict* itself. The pressure, especially from the educational system and mass media, on American Indians, especially the youth, to acculturate, a pressure which is opposed by their elders, leads to great stress for the youths.

A third theory focuses on the *breakdown of the family* in American Indian tribes. Parents are often unemployed, substance abusers and in trouble with the law, and divorce and desertion of the family by one or more parents is common.

Jilek-Aall (1988) asserted that the suicide rate among American Indians had risen greatly in recent years, and she attributed this to the imposition of rapid Westernization. She suggested that, when a society loses its traditional culture but is unable to achieve a satisfactory status in the new culture, a state of *anomic depression* results, a state involving anomie, cultural identity confusion, dysphoria, hopelessness and lack of self-respect. This is especially true for youth, and the impact of alcohol intoxication on the members of such a subculture is to facilitate violence and self-destructive behavior.

Jilek-Aall admits that suicide was present in traditional American Indian societies, among the elderly and infirm, to prevent capture in warfare, or as atonement. Suicides in the past were often honored. Youths today learn this from the stories told by their elders, and they hope for attention and acceptance in their deaths. Jilek-Aall also attributed the high incidence of self-destructive behavior in modern American Indian youth to the neglect, hunger, physical abuse, illness and bereavement to which they are frequently subjected.

Ogden, et al. (1970) listed a set of similar causes for the increase in American Indian suicide rates which they had noted: cultural conflict (stronger in the youth than in the older American Indians who have made peace with the two societies), alcohol abuse, broken homes, neglect of children, juvenile delinquency, truancy and school problems, poverty, geographic isolation, unemployment, cultural conflict, and difficulty in adjusting to a hostile environment.

Berlin (1987) suggested that the adolescent suicide rate in southwestern American Indian tribes was associated with the rate of alcoholism, drug and solvent abuse, child neglect and abuse, spouse abuse, auto accidents and homicides. The suicide rate appears to be higher in the less traditional and more acculturated tribes. However, probably the more acculturated tribes also have more chaotic families, alcohol abuse and child neglect. The high rates of both unemployment and menial employment may contribute to the high suicide rate, and often traditional American Indian values, such as not striving to be better than others, are in conflict with Anglo values in the larger society. Berlin also suggested that the practice of having American Indian children adopted by white families (he estimated that some 50,000 American Indian children have been adopted in this way) and sending

American Indian youths off to boarding schools increased their risk of suicide.

Durkheim's Theory

Durkheim (1897) proposed that the suicide rate of a society was determined by two broad social characteristics: the degree of social integration (that is, the extent to which people are bound together in social networks) and the degree of social regulation (that is, the extent to which the desires, aspirations and behavior of people are governed by social norms and customs). Suicide was more likely when the degree of social integration was too low (leading to *egoistic suicide*) or too high (leading to *altruistic suicide*) and when the degree of social regulation was too low (leading to *anomic suicide*) or too high (leading to *fatalistic suicide*).

Davenport and Davenport (1987) explored whether American Indian suicide fitted into Durkheim's (1897) typology for suicide. They argued that egoistic suicide (which results from a lack of social integration with others in the society) was probably not common in American Indians, either in the past or presently. The family and the tribe have always been very important to the American Indian, and their life was communal in nature. Despite the social disruption over the last two centuries, the family remains important, and their minority status may further reinforce their sense of community. Altruistic suicide may have been common in the past, both in the form of sacrifice during fighting in wars and in the custom in some tribes of the elderly staying behind by themselves to die as the tribe moves on. However, altruistic suicide is rarely, if ever, found today.

Anomic suicide[4] is the lack of regulation of the individual's emotions and desires by the culture, and Davenport and Davenport felt that this type of suicide was most common among American Indians today. The suppression of traditional Indian culture and the present clash of the traditional culture with the culture of the larger society has made it more common for the American Indian to feel normless.

---

[4] Davenport and Davenport did not consider fatalistic suicide.

Travis (1990) attempted to test Durkheim's assertion that the levels of social integration and social regulation in a society determine its suicide rate. He examined sociological correlates of the suicide rate among Alaska Natives from 1970-1984. Travis noted that, after the Federal Government settled the land claims of Alaska Natives in 1971, the suicide rate among Alaska Natives increased fourfold, reaching 90.8 per 100,000 per year among the [Inupiat] in the early 1980s. Travis suggested that this was due to the influx of Anglo-Americans into Alaska and the resulting culture-conflict among the Eskimo and to the lack of competitive skills possessed by the Eskimo, making them aspire to desire unattainable economic goals.

Despite his intent to test the usefulness of Durkheim's theory in explaining Eskimo suicide rates, Travis examined the effect only of age, gender, unemployment and marital status. Marital status is relevant to Durkheim's concepts of social integration and regulation, but the other variables are not. He found that suicide rates were higher for men, those under 30 and those unemployed. Only marital status was unrelated to suicide rates. Thus, Durkheim's theory, as phrased by Travis, was not supported by the data. Despite the inadequacy of Travis's report, his data do indicate that suicide rates are higher in young, male and unemployed Alaska Natives than in older, female and employed Alaska Natives.[5]

Travis (1984) reported a better study designed to explore whether Durkheim's theory could explain Eskimo suicide rates. Two groups of Eskimo [Inupiat] were studied, one from the North Slope centered around Barrow and one from the NANA region centered around Kotzebue. The Barrow region underwent an economic boom in the 1970s as the oil industry developed, while the Kotzebue region experienced an economic depression.

The Eskimo suicide rate in the Barrow region was 23.2 in 1960-1966, 23.7 in 1967-1973 and 19.2 in 1974-1980. In contrast the suicide rate for the Kotzebue region for these three time periods respectively was 0.0, 26.1

[5] For some obscure reason, Travis then examined the relationships between these same variables and suicide rates only for suicide committed on holidays and in new communities. These results are difficult to interpret since Travis seems to have reported his regression model incorrectly, asserting that the number of suicides on which the analysis is based is the same as for the previous analysis, even though the sample size has been greatly reduced.

and 106.0. Thus, the economically depressed region experienced a dramatic increase in the suicide rate. The two regions did not differ in level of education, household size, percentage unmarried and female labor force participation. In the Barrow region, however, a greater percentage of the population was employed by 1980 and the median family income was much higher.

None of these social variables were related to the Barrow region suicide rate from 1960-1980, whereas all but one were related to the suicide rate in the Kotzebue region. Suicide rates in the Kotzebue region were positively associated with education, being unmarried, income, and female labor force participation and negatively with the employment ratio. A multiple regression analysis identified employment, education and non-marriage as the three best predictors of the suicide rate in the Kotzebue region, and Travis (1985), in a re-analysis of his data, confirmed that unemployment and education adversely affected the suicide rate.

Durkheim argued that suicide rates would be higher during both economic booms and depressions. The data from these two regions suggest that only economic depressions are associated with suicide rates in these Alaskan Natives and that they serve to increase the risk of suicide.

May and Van Winkle (1994) collected together suicide rate for different American Indian tribes from diverse sources, and they then classified the tribes as low, moderate or high in social integration. The average rate of suicide for those tribes with high levels of social integration was 28.3, for those tribes with moderate levels of social integration 31.9, and for those tribes with low levels of social integration 56.9. (The medians were 18.5, 30.0 and 45.0 respectively.) Thus, suicide rates were high in the less socially integrated tribes.

Comment

Durkheim's theory provides a classification of types of suicide which may be useful for describing the type of suicide in American Indian tribes. Furthermore, the study by May and Van Winkle illustrates the potential usefulness of the concept of social integration for explaining the variation in suicide rates between tribes.

ACCULTURATION

Acculturation occurs when a culture encounters a more dominant alternative culture. The resulting pressure from the dominant culture leads to a variety of changes in the non-dominant culture which undergoes change (Berry, 1990): physical changes (such as type of housing, urbanization and increasing population density), biological changes (resulting from changing diet and exposure to new diseases), political changes (such as loss of autonomy for the non-dominant culture), economic changes (such as changes in type of employment), cultural changes (in language, religion, education and the arts), changes in social relationships (both within the culture and between the two cultures), and psychological changes at the individual level (in behavior, values, attitudes and motives).

Berry noted that four possibilities are open to the non-dominant culture:

integration
maintaining relations with the dominant culture
maintaining cultural identity

assimilation
maintaining relations with the dominant culture
not maintaining cultural identity

separation
not maintaining relations with the dominant culture
maintaining cultural identity

marginalization
not maintaining relations with the dominant culture
not maintaining cultural identity

It would be of great interest to categorize the different American Indian tribes as to which strategy appears to have been chosen and to examine the different consequences for the society and for the individuals in the society.

Does Cultural Conflict Cause Suicide?

The problem of acculturation has been proposed as one of the major causes of depression and suicidal behavior among American Indians. However, the majority of research reports on individuals who attempt or complete suicide mention precipitating causes such as grief over loss, quarrels with relatives and friends, etc. Rarely is cultural conflict listed among the precipitating causes. Of course, it may be that the problems of acculturation raise the stress level of individuals so much that stressors, which under ordinary circumstances would not precipitate suicide, now do so.

Occasionally brief case histories do appear which illustrate the problems of acculturation and culture conflict. Berlin (1986) describes cases in which the American Indian culture is the stressor. For example, a bright young woman who completed undergraduate school and qualified as a teacher was admitted to graduate school. Her clan, however, told her that she was required to teach on the reservation. Her desire to go to graduate school was seen as striving to be better than her peers, and this was unacceptable and forbidden. The young women had a psychiatric breakdown and was hospitalized. In a similar situation, the tribe and another family could not decide whether to let a young woman go to graduate school for an MBA after she obtained her undergraduate degree and, during the long wait for a decision, she attempted suicide.

In this latter case, the young woman, whom Berlin called Josie, had alcoholic parents who frequently sent her and her brothers and sisters to live with relatives while they went on drinking sprees. A teacher realized Josie's potential and received permission for Josie to live with her. With this teacher's help, her academic performance improved, and she went to college. Josie now resented that her parents who had neglected her were involved in decisions about her life. The clan leadership and tribal council was relatively enlightened about the issues and eventually gave permission for Josie to attend graduate school. While at graduate school, Josie underwent psychotherapy to deal with her depression and anger and other personal problems. After graduation, she returned to the tribe to manage their business office, marrying a young man who had fought a similar battle in order to obtain an MSW degree.

On the other hand, Westermeyer (1979) provided cases of American Indians seen at the University of Minnesota Hospitals for whom trying to live in the mainstream American culture had presented problems. Westermeyer felt that identity problems were perhaps no more common in American Indians than in whites, but that American Indians did show a unique type of identity problem, namely, ambivalent or negative feelings about their ethnic identity. Westermeyer presented ten urban American Indian cases which illustrated this problem, noting that they were not markedly different in demographic or clinical characteristics from other Indian patients.

Five of the patients, ranging in age from 12 to 23, had identity crises -- they experienced conflict about their Indian identity and about what being "Indian" meant. All were students and economically dependent upon others. For example, one young girl who was seen after a suicide attempt, had her Indian mother die two years earlier. She then lived with her white father and six siblings for a year. The father had trouble supporting them and sent the children to live with their Indian maternal grandmother. The patient began to use drugs and to have problems at school with her white teachers. Eventually a white welfare worker sent her to a white foster home, at which point she attempted suicide. In the hospital, she said, "I'm the only Indian here and I hate everybody like they hate me." She had a recurrent dream in which she gave birth to baby girl with blue eyes which she loved but which she also wanted to injure.

Five of the cases were judged to have a negative identity. These were older than the patients with identity crises, and all were male. They were estranged from their Indian family members, and they lived as lower class individuals on the periphery of the white society. One patient was admitted with hallucinations and paranoid delusions after a drinking binge. He had a record of multiple psychiatric admissions. Although he supported the idea of Indian activism, he felt estranged from Indians, had little respect for them and avoided them. He had joined a Jewish student activist group which he admired, and he wondered whether his Indian tribe might be a lost tribe of Israel. He identified himself as a Zionist.

In the adolescents, Westermeyer noted two different types of problems. The two boys were raised to assume a white middle class identity, but found this difficult because of their racial characteristics. The three girls were raised by Indian mothers who had rejected being Indian. Loss of their mothers, together with abandonment by their white fathers, led to anger. Their problems were made worse by social workers placing them in white foster homes.

Westermeyer noted that the negative identity in the adult patients served useful psychodynamic functions: (1) if their Indian relatives did not like them, then they could attribute this to that fact that these relatives were "bad," (2) it excused their bad behavior since they were "bad" Indians themselves, and (3) it led them to assume non-Indian "good" identities.

The majority of the urban Indians that Westermeyer studied were born on the reservation and often returned for visits and short stays. Thus, they were "part-time" immigrants to the city, unlike immigrants from foreign countries who were in the city more permanently. The kinds of problems American Indians faced were in some ways similar to those faced by others immigrants, such as Asians. However, less attention has been given by scholars to the problems facing American Indians than has been given to other ethnic groups.

Research on Acculturation

Everett (1975) noted that, although a common explanation of pathology, including suicidal behavior, in American Indians is that it is a result of acculturation, an alternative explanation is that pathology reflects long-standing traditional patterns of behavior. In order to confirm this second proposition, Everett noted that information is required on pre-reservation traditional behavior, early reservation behavior and contemporary behavior.

Everett attempted to explore these alternative propositions using data on suicide from two Apache tribes, White Mountain and [San Carlos]. In the mid-1870s both groups were placed on reservations. The San Carlos group was forbidden to travel, forced to become wage-laborers, and strictly supervised by an Apache police force. The police enforced local prohibitions of drinking, but the contact of the San Carlos Apaches with whites as a result of their labor led to bootlegging to obtain alcohol. Thus this group of Apache was oppressed and forced to acculturate.

The White Mountain Apaches remained nomadic and worked only voluntarily. They filled hay and wood contracts for the military, and they were not forced into wage-oriented labor. Supervision of the Apache was difficult due to their mobility over rough terrain. These Apache had little contact with whites.

Despite Everett's first requirement for testing the existence of traditional patterns of behavior, namely pre-reservation patterns, Everett admits that there are no reliable pre-reservation data on suicide and very little reliable data on early reservation suicide. His best estimates for suicide rates in the late 1800s are 9 for the San Carlos Apache and 9 to 21 for the White Mountain Apache. For the White Mountain Apache, the suicide rate rose from 9 for 1922-1931 to 32 for 1932-1941, peaking at 45 for 1952-1961 and dropping to 32 for 1962-1971. (Everett noted that, when the suicide rate increased in these decades, the homicide rate decreased and vice versa, suggesting that these two behaviors could be alternatives modes of expressing frustration.) For the San Carlos Apache, the only available rate was 42 for 1962-1971.

The pattern of suicide for the White Mountain Apache indicates a marked shift to females, younger adults, and singles during the 1900s. The precipitants have become predominantly arguments with spouses or kin. The men have typically used firearms and the women burning for suicide consistently.

The San Carlos Apache had a similar gender ratio distribution of suicides in the 1960s to that for the White Mountain Apache, but while the San Carlos Apache women also used burning for suicide, the men showed a greater variety in the methods for suicide as compared to the White Mountain Apache.

Everett tried to explain these results using the concept of acculturation. However, his data fail to support this explanation. Despite the differences in the cultural histories of the two groups on the reservation, their suicidal behavior shows remarkable similarity -- low in the late 1800s and rising in the

1900s. The pattern of suicide, at least in the 1960s for which comparable data are available, are also similar. On the other hand, the increase in the suicide rate from the 1800s to the 1900s, if valid, may be explainable using the concept of acculturation, assuming that the groups became more acculturated over this period, but Everett does not test this explanation in a methodologically sound manner. Furthermore, the recent decline in the suicide rate in the 1960s for the White mountain Apache, if valid, does not fit with an acculturation hypothesis, assuming that acculturation was continuing during this period.

Bagley (1991) looked at the suicide rate of Canadian Indian males aged 15 to 34 on the 26 most populated reservations in Alberta, Canada. He found that the suicide rates were positively associated with the level of poverty, a more northern latitude and distance from the nearest town with a population greater than 5,000. The suicide rate of young Indian males in the northern part of Alberta was 80.1, in the central region 71.2 and in the southern region 35.3. Thus, the more isolated reservations had the higher suicide rates. Bagley, et al. (1990) changed this study somewhat by including "careless" deaths in with suicidal deaths, deaths such as single car crashes, pedestrian deaths, and death from cirrhosis of the liver. The results were similar.

In contrast, Garro (1988) divided the province of Manitoba by the 53rd parallel; the northern communities are more remote, often inaccessible except by air in the winter, whereas the southern communities are more accessible. The suicide rate in the northern communities was 18.7 and in the southern communities 48.2. Looking at the suicide rate by tribe confirmed this difference: in the north, the Chipewyan had a suicide rate of 13 and the Ojibway [Northern] 5. The Cree in the middle of the province had a suicide rate of 22 and the Objibway (Salteaux) in the south had a rate of 48 and the Sioux 80. These results for Manitoba are in direct opposition to those of Bagley for Alberta.

Bachman (1992) looked at suicide in 120 counties in America which are partially or totally located on reservation land (so as to ensure a large population of American Indians) and studied the association of measures of economic deprivation (the percentage of American Indian families below the poverty line, the percentage of American Indians unemployed, and the percentage of American Indians aged 16 to 19 not enrolled in school and not high school graduates), social disorganization (the percentage of American Indians not living on the reservation in 1979 or 1980), and acculturation (the higher the percentage of American Indians on the reservation). Suicide rates were calculated for 1980-1987 and were found to be most strongly associated with the percentage of American Indians in the population, the percentage unemployed and the high school dropout rate. In a multiple regression analysis, unemployment, percentage of American Indians and percentage in poverty contributed significantly. If homicide rates were included in the analysis, the significant contributors included the homicide rate, poverty and unemployment. Thus, economic deprivation, rather than acculturation, seemed to be the strongest correlate of American Indian suicide rates in this study.

Van Winkle and May (1986) presented data on suicide in three groups of American Indians in New Mexico (the Apache, Navajo and Pueblo) and attempted to account for the differences in terms of the degree of acculturation. Van Winkle and May identified 317 suicides among native Americans in New Mexico from 1957 through 1979, 97 percent of which were committed by these three major groups.

Overall, the crude suicide rates were 43.3 per 100,000 for the Apache, 27.8 for the Pueblo, and 12.0 for the Navajo. The rates appeared to decrease from 1957 to 1965, rise precipitously from 1965 to 1975, and level off after 1975. The most common method for suicides for all three groups and both sexes was firearms.

Suicide was predominantly a male phenomenon, with a male/female ratio of about 9:1. The median age of the suicides was 26 years. All of the female suicides were aged between 10 and 44, and 81 percent of the male suicides between 10 and 39. Three-fourths of the Apache suicides were single as compared to 53 percent of the Pueblos and only 33 percent of the Navajo.

The suicides rates varied greatly between the individual reservations, tribes and villages. For example, the suicide rates for the period ranged from 56.6 for the Nambe reservation to 0.0 for the Sandia reservation. For the larger Pueblo tribes, Van Winkle and May compared the suicide rates of those tribes which had acculturated and those which had remained traditional and found a clear tendency for the acculturated (and transitional) tribes to have the higher suicide rates.

The Jicarilla and Mescalero Apache of New Mexico were originally nomadic hunters and gatherers, organized into self-sufficient bands whose leaders held limited power. Their religion had no organized priesthood and was not a cohesive force in their lives. Individualism was a highly valued characteristic. Today they live in homes scattered about the reservation or in border towns. They raise livestock, cut timber or work in tribally owned businesses. Formal tribal governments have been established, but religion remains unimportant. Individualism is still valued. However, the raiding parties which formerly provided a some degree of social integration have been eliminated. The Apache appear, therefore, to have few integrating forces in their culture, and Van Winkle and May saw their high suicide rate as a direct result of this lack of integration.

The Apache have been in contact with whites quite intensely. Their reservations are small and surrounded by white communities. Indeed many Apache live in mixed communities. Thus, the Apache have low social integration and high acculturation.

The Pueblo traditionally lived in compact towns and engaged in agriculture. Religion permeated their lives and was a strong integrating force. There was an organized priesthood and religious societies which took care of religious and civil matters. Individualism was discouraged and conformity valued. Thus, the Pueblo were the most integrated group, and Van Winkle and May find their intermediate suicide rate a puzzle. They try to explain the Pueblo having the second highest suicide rate using the concept of acculturation. The Pueblo have had increasing contact with whites from 1959 on. Many of the Pueblos are near large cities such as Albuquerque and Santa Fe. Thus, they have high social integration and moderate but increasing acculturation.

The Navajo, who have the lowest suicide rate, were nomadic hunters and gatherers who later settled down and turned to agriculture. They are organized into bands, but matrilineal clans exert a strong influence. Although religion is important in their lives, they have no organized priesthood. Individualism is valued but not as strongly as among the Apache. Thus, their social integration appears to be intermediate between that of the Apache and that of the Pueblo. However, the Navajo have been the most geographically and socially isolated from whites of the three groups until the 1970s when mineral exploration increased on their reservations and some Navajo began to take wage-earning jobs.

Van Winkle and May's explanation of the suicide rates in the three groups can be summarized as follows:

	social integration	**acculturation**	**suicide rate**
Apache	low	high	high
Pueblo	high	moderate	moderate
Navajo	moderate	low	low

Van Winkle and May used these two concepts (social integration and acculturation) to account for the suicide rates of the three native American groups, the changes in the rates over the years, and the variation among reservations within each group.

Van Winkle and May did not use the original Durkheimian formulation of the theory in which the relationship between social integration and suicide rates is curvilinear. Furthermore, Van Winkle and May did not consider the concept of social regulation to see if it would increase the explanatory power of their proposals. However, Van Winkle and May's study and interpretation have served to illustrate that acculturation may volume have explanatory power when applied to American Indian tribal suicide rates.

Can Only American Indians Counsel American Indians?

The issue of whether only "like" can counsel "like" effectively has been debated from many years. Do homosexual counselors work more effectively with other homosexuals, feminists with women, American Indians with

American Indians, etc.? Some have argued that good counselors can work effectively with any kind of client, but others have argued that any counselor could benefit from a better understanding of the client population. For example, counselors who work with one kind of problem, say alcoholism, probably improve as their experience of alcoholics increases. The same would be true of any client characteristic, including ethnicity.

Most counselors receive very little training in ethnic differences that would prepare them for working with clients of varying ethnicity's, and this is even more true for clients with suicidal problems on which even less has been written. Counseling tactics in general have to be adjusted for the cultural background of the client (Sue, 1981), and an awareness of the cultural stresses, values, beliefs, attitudes, experiences and language (both verbal and nonverbal) will enable the counselor to work more effectively with the client, especially if the client is identified with his or her ethnicity.

McIntosh and Santos (1984) noted the lack of information available about counseling suicidal American Indians. Some commentators have noted the modesty, humility, discretion and caution of American Indians which inhibits their involvement in counseling. American Indians, in general, value being a good listener and not criticizing others. They may also distrust whites in general and so be even more reluctant to open up with a white counselor. Richardson (1981) has suggested that a person-centered (nondirective, Rogerian) style of counseling may be more appropriate for American Indians, particularly at the beginning of the counseling process.

Preventing Suicide From A Cultural Perspective

Connors (1996) has presented the case of Robin, a thirteen-year Ojibway boy, adopted by white parents when he was two years old. From the time of his adoption, Robin had shown a great deal of anger and difficulty in forming healthy emotional attachments. He had destroyed property, set fire to the house, and killed a pet. In his teenage years, he lied, stole and used drugs. Connors recognized that these problems stemmed from his separation from and abandonment by his biological parents and that Robin felt alienated from the white culture into which he had been transferred.

Connors recommended that Robin join an Ojibway Adolescent Treatment Program. He was reintroduced to Ojibway cultural ways, and received counseling from an Ojibway counselor. He joined an Ojibway drum group and learned to sing in Ojibway and to dance Pow Wow. After some time in the program, he decided to go and live with his Ojibway extended family, and his counselors helped him make contact with them and move back. Connors continued to counsel him, and Robin's anger and self-destructive behavior soon disappeared.

Comment

The efforts made to explore whether acculturation could explain the variation in suicide rates between American Indian tribes have not been adequate or extensive yet. However, the research by Van Winkle and May on the tribes in New Mexico does suggest that such efforts might be rewarded. In contrast, however, the results from Alberta and Manitoba in Canada are inconsistent with each other, and a great deal of research is required to explain the different effects of acculturation and isolation on the suicide rates of the tribes in these two Canadian provinces.

The Effects of Age

Seiden (1981) focused on what we have observed earlier in Chapter 3, namely that American Indian suicide rates decline in older American Indians. Seiden noted that this pattern was similar to that found in African Americans and Hispanics, and different from that found in whites and Chinese Americans whose suicide rates continue to rise with age. Seiden suggested six reasons why American Indian suicide rates might peak at a young age.

(1) American Indians have a lesser life expectancy than whites, and perhaps only the strongest (physically and psychologically) American Indians survive into old age? (2) If suicide can validly be conceptualized in the oppressed as anger felt toward others directed inward onto the self (Henry and Short, 1954), then this aggressive behavior should, like other aggressive and

criminal behaviors decline with age -- a form of the "burn-out" which is found for alcohol abuse, drug abuse, traffic accidents, and crime. (3) In particular, those prone to violence (directed inward or outward) might have been killed early in life, either through murder or accidental deaths with a self-destructive component, such as motor vehicle deaths. (4) American Indian culture may provide more of a role for the elderly, thereby increasing their social integration above and beyond that found for whites who typically place a greater emphasis on the nuclear family and a lesser emphasis on the extended family. (5) Along with this, American Indians may accord the elderly more prestige in the community as well as condemning suicide more. (6) The precipitants for elderly suicide may differ from those for the young, and perhaps American Indian elderly experience fewer stressors than elderly whites? For example, elderly whites may experience much greater downward mobility (or fall from status) than American Indian elderly who were already at a relatively low status.

Markides and Machalek (1984) have presented a similar analysis, but in addition they do provide some evidence to support Seiden's first point above. Markides and Machalek noted that the mortality rate in general is lower in American Indians than in whites after the age of 75 (an even lower crossover age than is found for African Americans). Elderly American Indians over the age of 75 also have lower rates of hospitalization in nursing homes.

The Relative Cohort Size Theory

Easterlin (1980) suggested that the size of a birth cohort might have an impact on the behavior of the cohort. For example, the baby boomer generation was a large cohort and, as the members of this cohort became old enough to go to college and enter the work force, they would be competing for educational and career opportunities. The larger the cohort, the greater the competition for limited resources. Holinger (1987) applied this theory to the suicide and homicide rates of youths in America and found that the larger the size of the youth cohort (aged 15 to 24) as a proportion of the total population, the higher its suicide and homicide rate. Holinger speculated that a larger cohort of adolescents means increased competition for jobs, academic honors, and mental health resources. Thus, a larger cohort results in a larger proportion of youths who are psychologically vulnerable and fail to get external support for the self-esteem.

The American Indian population in the United States has risen dramatically in recent years, from 220,00 in 1900 to over 2,500,000 in 1980 (Berlin, 1987). The average age of the American Indian population is about 17.3 compared to 29.5 for America as a whole. Thus, the American Indian population has a very high proportion of adolescents and young adults. According to the relative cohort size theory of suicide, therefore, it is not surprising that the suicide rate is especially high among American Indian youth.

Studies of the Indian Health Service Areas

The Indian Health Service provides services for twelve areas: Aberdeen, Alaska, Albuquerque, Bemidji, Billings, California, Nashville, Navajo, Oklahoma City, Phoenix, Portland and Tucson. A number of studies have examined correlates of suicide (and homicide) rates over these twelve areas, research which is limited, of course, by the small sample size which makes obtaining statistically significant correlations difficult.

Young (1990, 1992a) found that suicide rates in 1979-1981 were positively associated with average household size and with the percentage of the population below the poverty level. (The homicide rate tended to be positively associated with both of these social indicators also, and was significantly associated with the suicide rate.) Young (1991b) found that the percentage below the poverty level was significantly associated with both suicide and homicide rates for men but not significantly associated with suicide and homicide rates for women.

Using data from 1974-1976 and only ten areas, Young (1991c) found that suicide rates (and homicide rates) were positively associated with the number of hospital beds available per capita of the population. Thus, the suicide rates did not vary by area because of inadequate medical facilities for treating injuries.

Using data from 1975-1977 and only eleven areas, Young (1991a) found that suicide rates were not associated with death rates from motor vehicle accidents or cirrhosis of the liver. Young (1992b) found that the sum of the suicide and homicide rates (which is often called the general aggression rate) and the suicide minus the homicide rate (commonly called a direction of aggression rate) were not associated over eleven of the areas with the deaths rates from accidents, heart diseases, malignant neoplasms, cirrhosis of the liver, influenza and pneumonia, cerebrovascular diseases, diabetes mellitus or all causes.

Overall, in the Indian Health Services regions, Young and French (1993) found that the suicide rate of American Indians was higher than that for Americans as a whole and peaked in the younger age groups (15 to 24 years of age), as we noted in Chapter 3 for American Indians in general. Thus, the suicidal behavior of American Indians is quite different from that of African Americans and, therefore, does not fit in with the predictions made for the suicidal behavior of oppressed groups made by Henry and Short (1954), who predicted higher homicide rates and lower suicide rates in the oppressed in a society since the oppressed would have clear external sources to blame for their misery. Thus, they should be angry and legitimately able to direct their anger outwardly.

Lester (1995) re-analyzed the data set utilized by Young in his studies, supplementing it with other social variables from the twelve Indian Health Service regions. Lester found that suicide rates were most strongly associated with the number of households in each region (negatively). In a backward multiple regression, suicide rates were predicted by the number of households (negatively) and poverty (positively). There was a difference by gender. Male suicide rates were most strongly associated with the number of households (negatively) and poverty (positively), while female suicide rates were not associated with any of the social variables. Thus, in this analysis, American Indian suicide rates were higher in the smaller and poorer regions.

OTHER RESEARCH

Cooper, et al. (1992) compared reservation areas in British Columbia (Canada) with high suicide rates for Canadian Indians and areas with low rates. The areas with high suicide rates had residents with less education, larger households, more children living at home, more single parents, fewer elders, and lower incomes generated by fewer people. Further analyses identified the following predictive signs of a high suicide rate: more than 4.3 persons per household, more than 10% of the households with six or more occupants, more than two children at home per family, less than 25% of the families having no children at home, more than 20% of the families headed by a single parent, more than 30% of the adult population (15 years and older) with a ninth grade education or less, less than 8% of the population aged 65 or older, and Indians constituting less than 5% of the off-reserve neighboring areas.

CONCLUSIONS

There has been a great deal of speculation about the causes of tribal suicide rates in American and Canadian Indians, but there has been very little sound research to test the validity of these explanations. There is some support for the relevance of acculturation stress and social integration in accounting for the tribal variation in suicide rates, at least in the United States. However, a great deal of further research is needed before we can be sure that these hypotheses have widespread relevance to American Indian suicide.

REFERENCES

Bachman, R. *Death and violence on the reservation.* New York: Auburn House, 1992.

Bagley, C. Poverty and suicide among Native Canadians. *Psychological Reports*, 1991, 69, 149-150.

Bagley, C., Wood, M., & Khumar, H. Suicide and careless death in young males. *Canadian Journal of Community Mental Health*, 1990, 9(1), 127-142.

Berlin, I. N. Psychopathology and its antecedents among American Indian adolescents. *Advances in Clinical Child Psychology*, 1986, 9, 125-152.

Berlin, I. N. Suicide among American Indian adolescents. *Suicide & Life-Threatening Behavior*, 1987, 17, 218-232.

Berry, J. W. Acculturation and adaptation. *Arctic Medical Research*, 1990, 49, 142-150.

Connors, E. A. The healing path. In A. A. Leenaars & D. Lester (Eds.) *Suicide and the unconscious*. Northvale, NJ: Jason Aronson, 1996, 259-269.

Cooper, M., Corrado, R., Karlberg, A. M., & Adams, L. P. Aboriginal suicide in British Columbia. *Canada's Mental Health*, 1992, 40(3), 19-23.

Davenport, J. A., & Davenport, J. Native American suicide. *Social Casework*, 1987, 68, 533-539.

Durkheim, E. *Le suicide*. Paris: Felix Alcan, 1897.

Easterlin, R. A. *Birth and fortune*. New York: Basic Books, 1980.

Everett, M. W. American Indian "social pathology." In T. R. Williams (Ed.) *Psychological anthropology*. The Hague: Mouton, 1975, 249-285.

Garro, L. C. Suicides by status Indians in Manitoba. *Arctic Medical Research*, 1988, 47, supplement 1, 590-592.

Holinger, P. C. *Violent deaths in the United States*. New York: Guilford, 1987.

Jilek-Aall, L. Suicidal behaviour among youth. *Transcultural Psychiatric Research Review*, 1988, 29(2), 87-105.

Lester, D. Suicide and homicide among Native Americans. *Psychological Reports*, 1995, 77, 10.

Markides, K. S., & Machalek, R. Selective survival, aging and society. *Archives of Gerontology & Geriatrics*, 1984, 3, 207-222.

May, P. A., & Dizmang, L. H. Suicide and the American Indian. *Psychiatric Annals*, 1974, 4(11), 22-28.

May, P. A., & Van Winkle, N. W. Durkheim's suicide theory and its applicability to contemporary American Indians and Alaska Natives. In D. Lester (Ed.) *Emile Durkheim: Le Suicide 100 hundred years later.* Philadelphia: Charles Press, 1994, 296-318.

McIntosh, J. L., & Santos, J. F. Suicide counseling and intervention with racial/ethnic minorities. In C. L. Hatton & S. M. Valente (Eds.) *Suicide assessment and intervention.* Norwalk, CT: Appleton-Century-Crofts, 1984, 175-194.

Ogden, M., Spector, M. I., & Hill, C. A. Suicide and homicides among Indians. *Public Health Reports*, 1970, 85, 75-80.

Richardson, E. H. Cultural and historical perspectives in counseling American Indians. In D. W. Sue (Ed.) *Counseling the culturally different.* New York: Wiley, 1981, 216-215.

Seiden, R. H. Mellowing with age. *International Journal of Aging & Human Development*, 1981, 13, 265-284.

Sue, D. W. (Ed.) *Counseling the culturally different.* New York: Wiley, 1981.

Travis, R. Suicide and economic development among the Inupiat Eskimo. *White Cloud Journal*, 1984, 3(3), 14-21.

Travis, R. More evidence on suicide and economic development among the Inupiat Eskimo. *White Cloud Journal*, 1985, 3(4), 31.

Travis, R. Halbwachs and Durkheim: a test of two theories of suicide. *British Journal of Sociology*, 1990, 41, 225-243.

Van Winkle, N. W., & May, P. A. Native American suicide in New Mexico, 1959-1979. *Human Organization*, 1986, 45, 296-309.

Westermeyer, J. Ethnic identity problems among ten Indian psychiatric patients. *International Journal of Social Psychiatry*, 1979, 25, 188-197.

Young, T. J. Poverty, suicide and homicide among Native Americans. *Psychological Reports*, 1990, 67, 1153-1154.

Young, T. J. Native Americans and the constant death instinct hypothesis. *Perceptual & Motor Skills*, 1991a, 72, 814.

Young, T. J. Suicide and homicide among Native Americans. *Psychological Reports*, 1991b, 68, 1137-1138.

Young, T. J. Medical resources, suicide, and homicide among Native Americans. *Corrective & Social Psychiatry*, 1991c, 37(3), 47-49.

Young, T. J. Household size, suicide, and homicide among American Indians. *International Journal of Comparative & Applied Criminal Justice*, 1992a, 16, 125-127.

Young, T. J. Mortality rates and aggression management among Native Americans. *Psychological Reports*, 1992b, 70, 665-666.

Young, T. J., & French, L. A. Suicide and social status among Native Americans. *Psychological Reports*, 1993, 73, 461-462.

Chapter 6

AMERICAN INDIAN SUICIDE AND HOMICIDE RATES IN THE STATES OF AMERICA IN 1980

An analysis of the mortality data tapes provided by the American government permits calculation of the suicide and homicide rates of the states by ethnic group (including American Indians). This chapter presents the results of some analyses of these data for 1980.

A COMPARISON OF AMERICAN INDIAN AND WHITE AMERICAN RATES

Lester (1994a) found that, for the 48 continental contiguous states of America in 1980, the white suicide rate was not associated with the American Indian suicide rate (Pearson r = 0.06); similarly, the homicide rates of American Indians and whites were not associated (r = 0.05). Only 25 states had American Indian populations over 10,000 in 1980. For this restricted sample of states, the rates of personal violence for American Indians and whites were not associated (r's = -0.05 for suicide and 0.03 for homicide). Thus, suicide and homicide rates of American Indians may be determined by different social variables than these rates for whites.

Suicide Rates in American Indians and Size of Population

Wechsler and Pugh (1967) predicted and found that individuals whose social characteristics are relatively uncommon in a community have higher rates of psychiatric breakdown. For example, Lester (1987b) found that the suicide rates of black residents in the states of America were higher in the states with fewer blacks residents. To explore whether this was true for American Indians, the data from 1980 were examined (Lester, 1994b).

The suicide rate of American Indians was not associated with the absolute number of American Indians in the 48 continental and contiguous states (Pearson r = 0.06) but was positively associated with the proportion of American Indian residents (r = 0.38, two-tailed p < .01). This result is in a direction opposite to that reported for African Americans. American Indian suicide rates were higher in states where there were relatively more American Indians. Restricting the analysis to the 25 states with more than 10,000 American Indians found similar results, with the correlations being -0.09 and 0.54 respectively.

Social Correlates of the American Indian Suicide and Homicide Rates[6]

Durkheim (1897), in his classic theory of suicide, predicted that social suicide rates should be greater in regions where indices of social integration (the degree to which people are bound together in social networks) and social regulation (the degree to which people's desires and emotions are controlled by social customs and norms) are either very high or very low. By extension, he anticipated that the following relationships should obtain: (1) low levels of social integration result in a type of suicide labeled by Durkheim as *egoistic*, (2) high levels of social integration result in a type of sui-

[6] This section is based on Lester (1995).

cide labeled by Durkheim as *altruistic*, (3) low levels of social regulation result in a type of suicide labeled by Durkheim as *anomic*, (4) high levels of social regulation result in a type of suicide labeled by Durkheim as *fatalistic*, and (5) moderate levels of both social integration and regulation result in relatively low suicide rates.

Johnson (1965) argued that the definitions of social integration and social regulation as offered by Durkheim and subsequent theorists, often overlapped, and that it made more sense to combine the two concepts into one. Furthermore, Johnson claimed, altruistic and fatalistic suicide are rarer than egoistic and anomic suicide. Therefore, he proposed simplifying Durkheim's theory, advancing a single, less complex proposition, namely, that lower levels of social integration/regulation lead to higher rates of suicide.

Many studies have confirmed predictions based on Durkheim's theory as modified by Johnson. For example, indicators of social integration/regulation, such as high divorce rates (which indicate low levels of social integration/regulation) have been shown to be positively associated with high suicide rates across states in the United States (Lester, 1988) and nations (Stack, 1981), and over time (Yang, 1992).

Henry and Short (1954) introduced homicide into this theoretical framework by arguing that the social stresses which lead to higher suicide rates also lead to lower homicide rates, and vice versa. This prediction springs from several assumptions, specifically that: (1) frustration results in aggression, (2) given strong external constraints on human behavior, frustrated people have external sources onto which to blame their unhappiness, thus legitimizing outward-directed aggression, leading to a high homicide rate, and (3) given weak external constraints on human behavior, frustrated people have no external sources onto which to blame their unhappiness, outward-directed aggression is thus not legitimized, consequently aggression is turned inward upon the self, leading to a high suicide rate.

Lester (1988) conducted a factor-analytic study of regional patterns of suicide and homicide at the state-level in the United States. He found that suicide rates varied negatively with a cluster of variables appearing to measure social integration/regulation (including divorce rates, alcohol consumption, church attendance, and interstate migration), and rates of suicide were less strongly associated with factors relating to longitude (suicide rates increased toward the west). Other analyses revealed that homicide rates varied positively with a cluster of variables appearing to measure southernness and less strongly with wealth (positively) and social integration/regulation (negatively). Lester concluded that these observations in regard to suicide supported the Durkheim/Johnson theory of suicide, since the strongest associations were between suicide rates and indices of social integration/regulation. However, the results with respect to homicide and suicide did not conform to Henry and Short's theory, since the associations between homicide rates and the social indicators were different from, but not opposite to those specific to suicide rates.

The analysis extends Lester's (1988) study to American Indian rates of personal violence measured at the state level. The overarching research questions were: Which states have higher rates of suicide and homicide for American Indians, and are these rates associated with indices of social integration? The patterns characteristic of American Indians were not expected to conform to those of the population as a whole since the former have been, and still are, an oppressed minority. Prior research suggests that the associations found for the dominant cultural group may not generalize to a minority group. For example, Lester (1990-1991) found that African American rates of suicide, at the state level, are quite different from those of whites. This raised the possibility, therefore, that the social correlates of American Indian suicide rates might differ substantially from those of whites.

Method

The data are for the year 1980 for the 48 contiguous, continental states of the USA. All data were obtained from the *Statistical Abstract of the United States*, published annually, and the *Census of the Population, 1980*, from the Department of Commerce, except for the following variables: suicide and homicide rates from mortality data tapes for 1980 supplied by the National Center for Health Statistics, the American Indian population from the Bureau of Indian Affairs, church attendance and percentage Roman Catholic (Quinn, et al., 1982), handgun control strictness (Lester, 1987a), alcohol consumption (Anon, 1985), gross state product per capita (Renshaw, et al., 1988), southernness (Gastil, 1971), and latitude and longitude (Lester, 1980).

State suicide and homicide rates for American Indians and for whites were calculated directly from the mortality data tapes for 1980 provided by the National Center for Vital Statistics. These rates are shown in Table 1.

A Factor Analysis

The state social variables were factor analyzed, using a principal components extraction with a varimax rotation (using SPSSx). The results are shown in Table 2. Eight eigenvalues were greater than one, and the SPSSx program extracted eight factors. Labeling factors is somewhat arbitrary, but was attempted on the basis of the social variables with the highest loadings (say, greater than .80 where possible): I *wealthy/urban* (median family income, per capita income, percent urban population, personal income), II *elderly* (birth rate, death rate, median age), III *southern* (percent black, southernness, latitude, percent married women working part-time), IV *social instability* (divorce rate, interstate migration, percent born in-state), V *unemployment* (male, female and total unemployment rate), VI *labor force participation* (females in labor force), VII *American Indian population* (American Indian population), and VIII *dense/Roman Catholic* (percent Roman Catholic and population density). Some of the labels describe the factors better than others, but are intended only to facilitate ease of reference in the discussion below.

Table 1. Suicide and homicide rates of Americans Indians per 100,000 per year, 1980 (calculated by the present author)

	population	suicide rate	homicide rate
AL	7561	0.00	0.00
AZ	152857	19.63	20.93
AR	9411	0.00	10.63
CA	201311	4.47	8.44
CO	18059	16.61	27.69
CT	4533	0.00	0.00
DE	1330	0.00	0.00
FL	19136	5.18	15.53
GA	7619	13.13	13.13
ID	10521	19.01	9.50
IL	16271	0.00	0.00
IN	7835	25.53	0.00
IA	5453	0.00	18.34
KS	15371	6.51	13.01
KY	3610	0.00	0.00
LA	12064	16.58	8.29
ME	4087	24.47	24.47
MD	8021	12.47	0.00
MA	7743	0.00	0.00
MI	40038	5.00	2.50
MN	35026	17.13	19.99
MS	6180	64.72	16.18
MO	12319	0.00	16.24
MT	37270	26.83	26.83
NE	9197	10.87	32.62

Table 1 (Continued)

NV	13304	15.03	37.58
NH	1352	0.00	0.00
NJ	8394	0.00	0.00
NM	104777	15.27	21.00
NY	38732	5.16	12.91
NC	64635	9.28	20.11
ND	20157	39.69	29.77
OH	12240	8.17	0.00
OK	169464	6.49	12.98
OR	27309	7.32	7.32
PA	9459	10.57	10.57
RI	2898	0.00	0.00
SC	5758	0.00	17.37
SD	45101	35.48	33.26
TN	5103	0.00	0.00
TX	40074	2.50	7.49
UT	19256	15.58	5.19
VT	984	0.00	0.00
VA	9336	0.00	0.00
WA	60771	16.46	19.75
WV	1610	0.00	0.00
WI	29497	13.56	6.78
WY	7125	28.07	42.11

Table 2. Results of the factor analysis (decimal points are omitted from the factor loadings)

	I	II	III	IV	Factor V	VI	VII	VIII
divorce rate	03	-16	-16	84#	02	06	10	-13
interstate migration	01	-28	05	87#	-28	08	04	01
church attendance	-23	-19	17	-65#	-39	-23	-08	29
gun control strictness	23	19	-01	-64#	18	19	06	07
alcohol consumption	34	13	28	55#	-12	35	-01	27
% born instate	-40	03	-07	-81#	12	-10	-20	-12
% foreign born	69#	31	05	04	07	-05	34	39
% Roman Catholic	50#	32	46	-02	06	-02	01	49
median family income	90#	-07	28	-05	03	19	-15	-03
per capita income	92#	16	24	06	-10	14	-04	-06
% urban population	83#	-04	-13	05	-02	-08	20	34
population	56#	21	-29	-33	23	-05	39	-13
population density	47	36	03	-31	05	-04	-24	55#
% in poverty	-64#	-06	-57#	-10	08	-16	21	06
gross state product	60#	-33	08	26	-32	-04	-03	-30
personal income	91#	19	24	12	-09	16	-02	-04
crime rate	65#	03	-14	47	13	13	27	32
% black	-07	05	-87#	-22	16	16	-16	09
southernness	-20	-10	-85#	18	16	-05	09	-26
latitude	06	03	90#	-09	10	19	-04	-10
infant mortality	06	18	-77#	-28	18	-02	-17	16
birth rate	-16	-90#	03	12	-18	-17	14	-09
% elderly	-20	75#	16	-18	-17	-44	07	02
% voting for Reagan	03	-56#	20	29	-46	-23	12	-05
longitude	08	-50#	14	42	-05	-04	50#	-32
death rate	-20	81#	-03	-28	-01	-38	-10	-02
% children	-34	-90#	-06	-03	05	-12	-01	-02
median age	26	93#	01	04	01	-14	-04	06
females/males	-02	58#	-31	-49	22	-16	-16	37
unemployment	-03	02	-07	-10	96#	-15	-05	01
male unemployment	03	04	06	-13	92#	-17	03	-07
female unemployment	-10	-03	-26	-04	89#	-08	-17	12
females in labor force	26	-08	35	09	-36	76#	-10	05
males in labor force	39	-42	41	04	-36	53#	-14	-08
employment ratio	21	-21	35	08	-52#	59#	-11	-08
married women working:								
full time	-21	-05	-58#	22	-29	61#	-04	-10
part time	23	-04	86#	-19	-17	21	-09	19
AmInd population	17	-08	-07	08	-04	-03	91#	-06
% AmInd population	-24	-26	20	24	-23	-15	63#	11
% of variance	25.2%	21.1%	12/5%	8.1%	7.6%	5.9%	3.3%	2.9%

a high loading of the variable on the factor (> 0.50)

The Pearson correlations between the SPSSx-derived factor scores for each factor and American Indian and white suicide as well as homicide rates are shown in Table 3. White suicide rates were associated with *social instability* and *American Indian population.* In contrast, the suicide rates of American Indians were associated with *wealthy/urban* and *elderly.* Since many states have few American Indian residents, the correlations were repeated using the subset of 25 states with 10,000 American Indian residents or more in 1980. Only the correlation of American Indian suicide rates with *wealthy/urban* was replicated on this reduced sample of states.

Table 3. Correlations of factor scores with rates of personal violence

	Factor							
	I	**II**	**III**	**IV**	**V**	**VI**	**VII**	**VIII**
All States:								
AmInd suicide rate	-0.29*	-0.36*	0.10	0.09	-0.12	-0.02	0.13	-0.03
White suicide rate	0.08	-0.21	-0.17	0.75*	0.03	-0.02	0.33*	-0.03
AmInd homicide rate	-0.13	-0.17	0.16	0.38*	-0.43*	0.03	0.23	-0.23
White homicide rate	0.16	-0.09	-0.61*	0.39*	0.09	-0.12	0.39*	0.09
25 States:								
AmInd suicide rate	-0.63*	-0.29	0.56*	0.06	-0.31	0.02	0.05	0.20
White suicide rate	0.19	-0.06	-0.33*	0.84*	0.03	0.02	0.21	0.40*
AmInd homicide rate	-0.42*	0.15	0.22	0.46*	-0.44*	0.27	0.16	0.09
White homicide rate	0.36*	0.07	-0.66*	0.44*	-0.01	-0.12	0.37*	0.33*

* statistically significant at the 5% level or better

There were more similarities in the patterns of homicide of whites and American Indians. For the full sample of 48 continental states, white homicide rates were associated with *southern, social instability* and *American Indian population.* (The association with *American Indian population* is rather puzzling. However, other social variables load on this factor, including longitude. It may be the contribution of these other variables which causes the association.) American Indian homicide rates were associated with *social instability* and *unemployment*. Thus, white and American Indian homicide rates shared an association with indices of social instability.

Using the reduced sample of states with larger American Indian populations, the association of American Indian homicide rates with social instability and unemployment were replicated.

Regression Analysis with the Eight Factors

The eight factor scores were used in a multiple regression analysis to predict American Indian and white suicide and homicide rates. The results are shown in Table 4. From an examination of the R^2 scores, it is evident that the factors were more successful in accounting for the white suicide rate than the American Indian suicide rate (76% and 26% of the variance, respectively), and similarly for homicide rates (73% and 51% of the variance, respectively).

Table 4. Results of the multiple regression over the 48 states using the eight factor scores: beta coefficients are shown

	Factor							
	I	II	III	IV	V	VI	VII	VIII
AmInd suicide rate	-0.29*	0.11	0.36	0.09	-0.12	-0.02	0.13	-0.03
White suicide rate	0.08	-0.17*	0.21*	0.75*	0.03	-0.02	0.33*	-0.03
AmInd homicide rate	-0.14	0.16	0.17	0.38*	-0.43*	0.03	0.23	-0.23*
White homicide rate	0.16	-0.61*	0.09	0.38*	0.09	-0.12	0.39*	0.09

Because of the small number of states (48) and the large number of social variables (39), the factor-analysis is of questionable validity. A second multiple regression was run, therefore, using the eight social variables with the highest loadings on each of the eight factors (per capita income, median age, latitude, interstate migration, unemployment, female labor force participation, American Indian population, and total population). The multiple R^2 scores were generally a little lower for these eight social variables than for the eight factor scores: American Indian suicide rates (26%), American

Indian homicide rates (44%), white suicide rates (73%) and white homicide rates (70%). However, the reduced success of these social variables in accounting for the American Indian rates of suicide and homicide was replicated in this set of analyses.

Discussion

The present study of statewide American Indian suicide rates reveals a very different pattern of associations in contrast to white statewide suicide rates. Whereas white suicide rates were associated with a cluster of variables that seem to measure social instability (thereby confirming Durkheim's theory of suicide), American Indian suicide rates were associated with a cluster of social variables that included measures of wealth and urbanization. American Indian suicide rates were higher also in the poorer/less urban states, probably a result of the large reservations being in those states and higher suicide rates among American Indians on reservations.

In contrast, the homicide rates of American Indians and whites showed some similarities in their pattern. Both were associated with social instability, with states which had greater social instability also having higher homicide rates for both whites and American Indians. In addition, American Indian homicide rates were higher where general overall unemployment is lower.

The present analysis indicated, therefore, the importance of examining whether the "classic" theories and research findings for suicide and homicide apply to all groups. The results reported here suggest that alternative theories may be required to account for rates of personal violence among American Indians. For example, Van Winkle and May (1986) examined the influence of social integration and acculturation on suicide rates in a small number of American Indian reservations in New Mexico. Their work indicates that acculturation plays a larger role in predicting suicide rates than does social integration.

Future research should explore the potentially predictive social variables in regard to suicide and homicide rates of American Indians living on and off reservations. It also would be useful to determine whether certain social indicators specific to American Indians have better success in predicting suicide and homicide rates. It is hoped that the present analysis will stimulate further sociological study of American Indian suicide and homicide rates.

Conclusions

The state suicide rates of American Indians in 1980 showed a very different pattern of associations with state social variables than did the state suicide rates of whites. In contrast, the homicide rates had similar associations, in particular with an index of social instability. The implications of these findings for theory are examined, and suggestions made for further research.

References

Anon. *US apparent consumption of alcoholic beverages based on state sales, taxation, or receipt data.* Rockville, MD: National Institute on Alcohol Abuse and Alcoholism, 1985.

Durkheim, E. *Le Suicide.* Paris: Felix Alcan, 1897.

Henry, A. F., & Short, J. F. *Suicide and homicide.* New York: Free Press, 1954.

Gastil, R. Homicide and a regional culture of violence. *American Sociological Review*, 1971, 36, 412-427.

Johnson, B. D. Durkeim's one cause of suicide. *American Sociological Review*, 1965, 30, 875-886.

Lester, D. Variation of suicide and homicide by latitude and longitude. *Perceptual & Motor Skills*, 1980, 51, 1346.

Lester, D. An availability-acceptability theory of suicide. *Activitas Nervosa Superior*, 1987a, 29, 164-166.

Lester, D. Social deviancy and suicidal behavior. *Journal of Social Psychology*, 1987b, 127, 339-340.

Lester, D. (1988). A regional analysis of suicide and homicide rates in the USA. *Social Psychiatry & Psychiatric Epidemiology*, *23*, 202-205.

Lester, D. Mortality from suicide and homicide for African Americans in the USA. *Omega*, 1990-1991, 22, 219-226.

Lester, D. Native American suicide and homicide rates. *Psychological Reports*, 1994a, 74, 702.

Lester, D. Suicide rates in Native Americans by state and size of population. *Perceptual & Motor Skills*, 1994b, 78, 954.

Lester, D. Social correlates of Native American suicide and homicide rates. *American Indian and Alaska Native Mental Health Research*, 1995, 6(3), 46-55.

Quinn, B., Anderson, H., Bradley, M., Goetting, P., & Shriver, P. *Churches and church membership in the US, 1980*. Atlanta: Glenmary Research Center, 1982.

Renshaw, V., Trott, E. A., & Friedenberg, H. L. Gross state product by industry. *Survey of Current Business*, 1988, May, 30-46.

Stack, S. Suicide and religion. *Sociological Focus*, 1981, 14, 207-220.

Van Winkle, N. W., & May, P. A. Native American suicide in New Mexico, 1959-1979. *Human Organization*, 1986, 45, 296-309.

Yang, B. The economy and suicide. *American Journal of Economics & Sociology*, 1992, 51, 87-99.

Chapter 7

SUICIDE IN DIFFERENT TRIBES

Many studies, both statistical and descriptive, have appeared on suicidal behavior in specific American Indian tribes, and this research will be reviewed in the present chapter. The chapter is organized by tribe, in alphabetical order.

APACHE (WHITE MOUNTAIN/COYOTERA)

Levy and Kunitz (1969) tried to answer two questions about suicide in the White Mountain Apache: was the suicide rate high, especially after the tribe settled on the reservation, and was this due to acculturation stress? However, their data did not permit them to answer either of these questions.

From 1965-1967, there were only three suicides in a population of about 5,000, giving a suicide rate of about 20.0. But such a rate is quite unreliable based on a small population studied for only a short period of time. Two of the suicides were female, and two were accomplished by self-immolation with kerosene. In 1967, there were nine attempted suicides seen at the Public Health Service Hospital, all by overdose and involving seven women and two men.

Levy and Kunitz cite Hrdlicka (1908) who reported about one suicide a year, giving a rate of about 50, but this is an even cruder estimate than that provided by Levy and Kunitz for 1965-1967. They also cite an unpublished paper by Bartell (1964) who noted 28 completed and attempted suicides (he did not specify how many of each) for the period 1946-1961 and who suggested that the high suicide rate was a post World War Two phenomenon. It can be seen that estimating suicide rates for a small population is a very difficult task without long-term reliable data.

Everett (1970) noted that the White Mountain Apache do not consider completed suicide to be predictable (although after a suicide attempt they expect further attempts). Typically suicide is motivated by the desire for revenge on others who are then later held to blame for the victim's suicide. Although many deny their guilt, many assume responsibility and punish themselves, sometimes leaving the reservation. Suicide is a very disruptive act in the community, engendering both grief among the survivors and guilt in the offenders, and there is some degree of disapproval of (or intolerance for) suicide in the society. However, after examining nine different types of pathology in the society, including suicide, Everett was not able to find any association between the degree of disruption generated by the pathological act and the intolerance of the society toward it.

Everett, et al. (undated) imply, without presenting good data, that adult White Mountain Apache often attempt suicide when drunk, unlike the teenagers. However, attempted suicide is common among teenagers, typically as a coercive tactic as a result of feeling oppressed.

Blackfoot

Anon (1970) reported on suicidal behavior among the Blackfoot Indians in Montana. Fatal and nonfatal suicidal behavior was quite frequent. In an eight-month period, there were 55 suicide attempts and five suicidal fatalities in a population of 6,000 American Indians, spread over 1.5 million acres, half of them under twenty years of age.[7] Three-quarters were female, the modal age was 12 to 21 (especially 15 to 17), and most had sought help in the two weeks prior to their suicidal behavior.

A crisis center had been established by a nurse, Audra Pambrum, herself a Blackfoot Indian. She set up a telephone crisis counseling service combined with a walk-in clinic since many of the Indians did not own telephones. The service was staffed by Ms. Pambrum and community aides whom she had trained.

The anonymous author claimed that suicide was unheard of in the past and saw the recent epidemic as a result of the culture conflict between the American Indian culture and mainstream American culture. How can the American Indian youth be successful while still remaining American Indian? There are few models for youths to imitate.

The clients seen by the crisis service were not the poorest of the reservation, but from a borderline group just above the poverty line. Their parents and the youths themselves had set goals, but they had come to see that they would not achieve the goals, a result of prejudice toward American Indians, disillusionment about school and a lack of job opportunities. Their failure led to helplessness and hopelessness, and many turned to alcohol to relive their depression.

CHEROKEE AND LUMBEE

Humphrey and Kupferer (1982) compared suicidal behavior in the Cherokee and Lumbee in North Carolina. The Cherokee primarily reside on a reservation in two counties and have both conservative and acculturated groups. The Lumbee do not have their own language or reservation and have intermarried extensively while retaining their ethnic identity.

The suicide rate among the Cherokee rose (by 170%) from 1972-1973 to 1974-1976, from 11.5 to 31.1, while the suicide rate in the counties as a whole decreased (from 17.5 to 9.9). The suicide rate in the Lumbee rose a

[7] The completed suicide rate is, therefore, roughly 125 per 100,000 per year.

little during the same period, from 8.3 to 10.3, while the rate in their counties as a whole increased rather more (from 9.5 to 14.7). (Kupferer and Humphrey [1975) reported the Cherokee suicide rate to be zero in 1972 and 23 in 1973 and the Lumbee suicide rate to be 3.6 in 1972 and 13 in 1973.)

For the Cherokee, suicide was found only in those aged less than 35 years of age. Although suicide rates among the Lumbee were higher in the older age groups, there was an increase in the suicide rate of younger Lumbee (under the age of 35) from the first to the second period.

Interestingly, the homicide rate rose in the Cherokee over this period whereas the homicide rate in the Lumbee decreased. Thus, although these two groups may differ in many cultural traits, the more integrated Lumbee appear to have conformed more to the violent behavior of the larger society whereas the Cherokee, who were experiencing conflicting pressures, showed an increasing trend toward both more externally and more internally-directed violence.

Thurman, et al. (1985) obtained data on six adolescent Cherokee who attempted suicides (four girls and two boys). They used overdoses and cutting their wrists for their attempts, and the precipitants were most often sexuality and broken relationships with boyfriends and girlfriends. Cultural difficulties were not apparent, and the motivation for the attempts was similar to that for white adolescents.

CHEYENNE

Dizmang (1967) attributed the high rate of suicide among the Cheyenne [Northern] to a loss of ways for acquiring self-esteem and the disintegration of traditional ways of dealing with aggression. In the past, though suicide was rare in Cheyenne men, depressed men organized war parties and, during the ensuing battles, would either perform acts of bravery which restored their self-esteem, or died in battle (a form of suicide). Suicide was more common among Cheyenne women, stemming most often from unhappy, cruel or childless marriages.

In raising the children, the outward expression of aggression was forbidden, and children who aggressed were verbally shamed. The approved way of expressing anger was through mock battles with an "enemy," hunting buffalo, and self-mutilation behavior in the Sun Dance. After being confined to their reservation, the Sun Dance was forbidden, the buffalo became extinct, and fighting between groups banned. The Cheyenne men were forced to cut their long hair, and, because there were no means of support on the reservation, welfare programs were established. The resulting symptoms were alcoholism and violent deaths (from suicide, homicide and accidents).

Synthesizing the Cheyenne culture with American mainstream culture has proven difficult. The problems include communication since the children are raised to speak in the Cheyenne language, with English as a second language only. As the Cheyenne children learn the Cheyenne history, they are filled with anger toward the white ethnic group and contempt for their defeated ancestors. Yet the white world remains tempting, despite the fact that Cheyenne values view desertion of Cheyenne kin as a very serious cultural offense. If the Cheyenne decide to leave, there is no Cheyenne subculture in the major cities to which they can go and obtain support as they struggle to succeed in the white world.

Dizmang saw the traditional crisis services as of little value to the Cheyenne. For example, there were few telephones, and so a telephone crisis service was useless. Dizmang suggested identifying the gatekeepers in the Cheyenne community and training them to recognize and provide crisis intervention for those at risk for suicide. The possible gatekeepers included the clergy, VISTA volunteers, and community health workers. The backup resources could be the Public Health Service hospital staff, with the nearby Veterans Hospital as a further back-up.

Those Cheyenne who wish to leave the reservation must be trained in such a way that they will succeed in the white world. They must acquire the education and skills which are necessary, and they must be taught the work habits of the white world, habits which are alien to them. Dizmang noted that a Neighborhood Youth Corps had been quite successful in this regard.

In the 1960's, those Cheyenne who wished to stay on the reservation were dependent upon welfare. It was necessary to create jobs on the reservation and provide leisure pursuits to lessen the reliance on drinking alcohol. Rather than such activities being imposed on the Cheyenne, Dizmang felt that they should come from the community itself so that they will be more acceptable to the Cheyenne.

Barter and Weist (1970) reported on the Cheyenne [Northern] living on a reservation in southeastern Montana. In 1967, four young adults committed suicide in a period of only ten weeks. In order to understand this epidemic, Barter and Weist studied the suicidal patterns back to 1830. From 1830-1883, a period before the Cheyenne were moved to the reservation, there were several suicide patterns. (1) Suicidal warriors fought in such a way as to die in battle, for example, by tying themselves to a stake so that they could not escape, or by charging into the enemy again and again. (2) Suicide, particularly among women, was associated with a loss of prestige. If the woman was humiliated in some way, her suicide released her from the pain of the humiliation and made the perceived aggressor guilty. (3) The Cheyenne, both men and women, also committed suicide after losing a loved one. (4) Finally, sometimes the Cheyenne committed suicide because of the difficult situation they found themselves in, as after attacking and killing white soldiers. In this period, the women typically died by hanging, and their interpersonal conflicts were usually with other women (mothers, sisters and sisters-in-law). Men most often chose to die in battle, and sometimes loss of a brother was the precipitating event. There were no cases of husbands committing suicide because of conflicts with their wives.

During the reservation period, from 1884-1949, the Cheyenne switched to farming, and Christian schools were established. The farming failed, and the Cheyenne were soon reduced to depending upon government welfare. There were fewer suicides during this period, especially among the women. The elimination of warfare also led to the disappearance of the suicidal warrior pattern for male suicides. The situation of women seems to have improved during this period. They were less often tied to their mother's home, and the elimination of sororal polygyny led to fewer conflicts with sisters. Boarding schools offered young girls a chance to escape from their mothers' domination.

In the contemporary period, from 1950-1968, there was a marked increase in suicide among the men. These suicides often occurred after conflict with their wives. From the wives' point of view, their husbands are unemployed, lazy and drink too much in the company of other men. The men have low self-esteem, and rejection by their wives worsens their psychological state. The husband's suicide often leads to the wife being blamed for precipitating her husband's death by criticizing him too much. Homicide followed by suicide has now also appeared among the Cheyenne, a pattern unknown in pre-reservation times.

In this period, there has also been increased contact with the white culture. Cheyenne men served in the Second World War and the Korean War, and this broadened their horizons. A road was built through the reservation which increased access both on and off the reservation, and television brought the outside world into view. This has served to raise the aspirations of the Cheyenne without providing them with increased opportunities for realizing these aspirations. However, the Cheyenne themselves see the increased suicide rate to be a result of alcohol abuse and the mishandling of the tribal fetish, that is, a failure to follow the cultural rituals properly.

Barter and Weist also reported on deaths in general in this group of Cheyenne. From 1963-1967, there were 137 deaths among a population of some 2,300 Cheyenne, giving an annual death rate of about 1,000. Suicide was the fifth leading cause of death (4% of all deaths). They calculated suicide rates for the whites and Cheyenne of two counties (Big Horn and Rosebud) each decade from 1910-1968. By decade the white suicide rate was 8, 12, 20, 15, 12 and 17 (the last rate is for a nine-year period); the Cheyenne suicide rates were 22, 21, 13, 6, 40 and 48. Only for 1930-1949 did the white suicide rate exceeded the Cheyenne suicide rate, perhaps because the Great Depression had less of an impact on the already impoverished Cheyenne.

As far as attempted suicide is concerned, this was rare in the pre-reservation period, but it has become more common since then. From 1963-1967, there were 40 recorded suicide attempts, 23 by women and 17 by men. For the married women, the attempts usually occurred after conflict with the husband, and the motivation was to invoke guilt in the frustrator.

Similarly, the attempts by men were often after conflict with women. Interestingly, the average age for the suicide completers was 26.8 and for the attempters 25.2, quite similar.

ESKIMOS

Foulks (1980) noted that Eskimos typically have two primary motives for suicide: becoming infirm and the loss of kin. Foulks suggested that suicide, alcohol use and traditional dissociative states serve a similar function for Eskimos, namely, escaping feelings of being socially worthless and dealing with having to suppress frustration and anger.

In the past, frustration and resentment, feelings which are not useful for the cooperative spirit which life in the Arctic demands, were released by means of the ritual catharsis of songs and dances and, more directly, during shamanistic seances during which the individual might go into a trance, behave violently toward the self and others, have a seizure and then have amnesia for the entire experience.

In modern times, drunken intoxication has begun to take the place of these seances, even though drinking is also used to promote sociability and congeniality. Foulks attributed these patterns to child rearing experiences in which the children are permitted a high level of gratification of dependency needs, the emphasis on cooperation, and cultural norms (which, for example, include beliefs in soul loss, supernatural possession and loss-of-control behavior models). Today, drinking is used to relieve depression, but drinking in turn leads to greater depression and apathy, with self-hatred and suicide at the end.

Leighton and Hughes (1955), studying the Eskimos (St. Lawrence Island), noted that suicide was supported by cultural norms in this group, especially for the elderly who could contribute no more to the society. The souls of suicides (and those dying from other forms of violent death) were thought to go to the best afterworlds. Historically, the most common methods of suicide were stabbing, shooting, hanging, jumping, drowning and starvation. In general, suicidal behavior was non-ritualized, that is, it was carried out by individuals in their own way, with only the motives for the suicide supported by social norms, the most common of which were physical and mental suffering and no longer being useful to the society.

In the St. Lawrence Island Eskimos, the pattern of suicide was a little more ritualized than ordinarily found, resembling more the suicidal behavior of the Chukchee on the neighboring mainland of Siberia. Leighton and Hughes obtained data from informants on 15 completed suicides, together with fragmentary information about 29 other suicides, most of whom were men. The last suicide about whom they had information occurred in 1902.

The most common methods were, in order, hanging, shooting with a rifle and stabbing. It was common for the victim to request being killed by others. The suicide first asked relatives to kill him, and they typically would not consent to do so at first but try to persuade him not to die. However, eventually they had to agree. The suicide would then dress himself as one already dead, that is, with his clothes inside out. His relatives would then carry him on a deerskin to the killing grounds (though it was also considered praiseworthy if the man walked to this place). The suicide made a death speech, advising his relatives and reflecting upon his life, after which a relative would kill him in a ritualized manner. The body was then buried in the traditional manner. The executioner had a cleansing ritual to endure, including confinement to the house for twenty days, wearing the same clothes, and shaving the head and eyebrows without water. These restrictions were more severe than those for the survivors of a person dying from other causes. (Since helping a person to commit suicide by hanging required the assistance of several relatives, the restrictions were not quite as severe in these cases.)

The motives for suicide included suffering due to a physical illness, prolonged grief over the death of a significant other, and chronic depression. Leighton and Hughes also identified a motive for this group of Eskimos which they did not find in other groups, namely the belief that by committing suicide you could save the life of a sick son or grandson.

Although it was most commonly elderly men who committed suicide, Leighton and Hughes could find no evidence for the abandonment of the elderly. Leighton and Hughes felt that the suicides in this group of Eskimos could be described as *altruistic* in the Durkheimian (1897) sense, that is, the result of strong social integration of the individual into the society. Suicide relieves the suffering of the individual, but it also affords the suicide prestige. The society is relieved of a drain on its resources, yet murder is discouraged. Since the relatives are involved in the rituals of the suicide, the suicide serves to reinforce the kinship bonds. The ritualized punishment for aiding the suicide stresses the seriousness of the act and again reinforces the group solidarity.

HOPI

Levy and Kunitz (1971) reported the Hopi suicide rate from 1956-1965 to be 8. Levy and Kunitz (1987) reported rates from 1956 on: 1956-1965 8, 1961-1970 13, 1966-1975 14-30, 1971-1980 25-35, and the following three-year moving-averages 1981 24, 1982 23, 1983 14, 1984 13 and 1985 13. The peak suicide rate was typically for males aged 20-24.

Simpson, et al. (1983) calculated a suicide rate for the Hopi for 1979-1980 of 27, and suicides accounted for 38% of the deaths. The suicide rate peaked for those aged 15 to 24 at 118. They also noted 33 attempted suicides. Eleven of the suicidal acts occurred in the jail after arrests for intoxication.

Levy and Kunitz (1987) noted that the Hopi reservation consists of twelve villages, with about 7,600 residents in 1985, and the tribe splits into those supporting the traditional theocracy and those supporting the modern tribal council. Many Hopi have settled in three off-reservation towns. The tribe argues that alcohol abuse is a modern phenomenon, but Levy and Kunitz note that prior to the 1960's people drank privately (and rarely in public) and that the traditional villages expelled their alcoholics.

Marriage was typically within the village and between people of similar status. Increasingly, people have married those from different villages and intermarried with the Tewa (Pueblo). These marriages lead to problems in the matrilineal society and are labeled as deviant by the Hopi. Levy and Kunitz found much more social pathology of all kinds among the children of these mixed marriages than among the children of traditional marriages.

Suicide can be precipitated by even the expectation of labeling. One man who wished to marry a woman from another tribe, but whose family refused to agree to the marriage, committed suicide. Levy and Kunitz describe the case of deviant mixed family whose father began to drink heavily and was pressured to move to one of the "progressive" villages. Here the father became a bootlegger, and his wife began to abuse alcohol. They moved to an off-reservation border town, and the children finished their education and found employment. The father's brother and family joined them. After several years, the father murdered his wife, and within two years two of the sons committed suicide and a daughter and niece began having hysterical attacks. The father died some years later of cirrhosis of the liver.

KWAKIUTL

Hochkirchen and Jilek (1985a) reported on two small isolated settlements of Kwakiutl. In a small island community, from 1963-1972 there were four suicides and from 1973-1982 sixteen, with suicide rates of 31 and 123 per 100,000 per year respectively. In a coastal community, the suicide rates for the two periods were 50 and 175 respectively. Sixteen of the suicides were men and 13 were women, and from 1973-1982, 19 of the 25 suicides were under the age of 30. The men used firearms most often while the women used overdosing.

Hochkirchen and Jilek felt that the Kwakiutl in these two communities, accessible only by plane or boat, were in a state of chronic dysphoria (or depression) and saw themselves as mistreated, infringed upon, disadvantaged and inadequate. They abused alcohol, typically in group binge drinking. Hochkirchen and Jilek called this psychological state *anomic depression.*

Suicide is made more acceptable by their attitudes which include a fantasy that a suicide attempt will magically change their lives should they survive. It is as if the "bad" self will die, leaving the "good" self to survive. Suicide also has an adventurous aspect, and substitutes for traditional ways of showing one's heroism. They can show courage by braving death. Suicide victims are viewed as martyred heroes. Their lives are glorified, and the funeral is a big social gathering which commemorates the life of the deceased. Thus, potential suicides can anticipate how they will be spoken of and glorified after their deaths. Finally, there is the belief that the dead are reunited with their loved ones in the life after death, which adds further motivation to the act. Suicide was also perhaps a way of gaining mastery over events in their lives.

Hochkirchen and Jilek noted that attempted suicide was common in these communities among middle-aged women, typically motivated by a desire to bring attention to their plight. Their families were usually severely disrupted, with abuse by the drunken male kin. The suicide attempt was seen as a sacrifice to obtain help for her family.

Mojave

Devereux (1942) described a form of suttee among the Mojave. The Mojave do not believe in a permanent afterlife. Rather the soul becomes a ghost in the land of the dead, where it repeats its previous life. After a few such metamorphoses, it ceases to exist. Therefore, the only way to remain with a deceased loved one is to die soon afterwards so that the ghosts may be together. Thus, funeral suicide is an attempt to achieve a meaningful reunion with the loved one. Funeral suicide only occurs after the death of a spouse or blood-relative (such as a son or parent), and never for a lover or friend. Funeral suicide is also consistent with the Mojave tendency to burn material possessions both of the deceased and the survivors at a funeral. The Mojave say that only women commit funeral suicide, but Devereux recorded several cases of men doing so. However, since the Mojave expect funeral suicide, they take such good precautions that almost all the individuals are saved. In fact, no successful suicide has ever been recorded. Thus, funeral suicide has become a socially useful and accepted outlet for pent-up emotions in the crisis of loss. Whereas other suicide attempters may be taunted and teased, those attempting funeral suicide are received with sympathy and commiseration.

NAVAJO

Wyman and Thorne (1945) collected data on 28 completed suicides and five attempted suicides among the Navajo from 1878 to 1942, though it is difficult to be sure that they located every suicide during this period. They noted that their informants claimed that suicide was rare among the Navajo, but Wyman and Thorne did not attempt to calculate a suicide rate for the Navajo. The majority of the suicides were in the upper age ranges and male, and the act was usually committed at home.

The most common method was by firearm, with hanging ranked second. Wyman and Thorne were struck by the complete absence of poisoning as a method despite the presence of plants such as Jimson weed in the region. As far as motives for the suicide, Wyman and Thorne noted five cases where grief over dead relatives seemed salient. Marital troubles were the precipitating cause for four suicides, and family quarrels in five murder-suicides. In ten cases, avoidance of capture and punishment by whites was the precipitant -- after eight murders, one theft of cattle and one rape of a little girl. In four cases the suicide was incurably ill. Wyman and Thorne noted that these precipitating factors were similar to those traditionally given for white suicides, except that financial motives (common in whites) and revenge for mistreatment (common in some Indian tribes such as the Iroquois) were absent.

Wyman and Thorne's informants seemed to take a casual attitude toward suicide. Suicides were seen as unfortunates who could have lived longer if they had behaved differently. The act was not condemned, though it was not condoned. However, suicides are prevented from associating with others in the spirit world, according to Navajo beliefs, and they must continually carry with them the implements which they used for suicide. Suicides are buried with the same ceremonies as those dying from natural causes, and their ghosts can return as can those of other deceased Navajos.

Levy (1965) reviewed the data presented by Wyman and Thorne and found problems. For example, they list four suicides from 1940-1944, while the local police departments have records of five. Only one name appears on both lists, so the incidence of suicide among the Navajo during this period is obviously greater than either source would estimate.

Levy noted that tribal police records indicate an increasing suicide rate from 1954 to 1963. The suicide rate peaked in 1961 at 16.1 per 100,000 per year. In 1962, the suicide rate was 9 and the ten-year average was 8.3. Levy noted that the suicide rate for the Navajo during this period (8.3) was lower than the rates for the states of Arizona (11.6) and New Mexico (11.5), the nation as a whole (10.6), and the rates for the Apache (Mescalero and Jicarilla combined) (20.8), Pueblos [Eastern/New Mexico] (10.2).

Navajo males were 13 times more likely than females to complete suicide and also led in attempted suicide by a ratio of 28:1. In this the Navajo resemble the Pueblos, and Levy suggested that the matrilineal clan systems and matrilocal residence patterns may provide greater social integration for Navajo women than for men. Suicide was most common in those aged 25 to 39, the rate peaking in those aged 35 to 39 and declining rapidly thereafter. The modal Navajo suicide is a young married man with children, with firearms followed by hanging as the most common method. Since 1945, Levy felt that the suicides had become younger.

Unlike Wyman and Thorne, Levy did find some suicides using poisons, mainly women and mainly attempted suicides. Suicide was most common at or near the home. The most common motives remained marital problems and jealousy, with intra-familial discord the second most common precipitant. Depression and alcohol intoxication appeared to be more common in recent suicides than in the past. About 47 percent of the suicides were intoxicated with alcohol at the time of the suicide, which is more than the percentage reported by Wyman and Thorne but, since many of their cases were reports of suicides from earlier times by informants, their data on this may be incomplete. Wyman and Thorne found that 38 percent of the suicides were murder-suicides, while Levy found that only 7 percent of his cases were murder-suicides. Levy felt that many of the suicides were impulsive, violent eruptions of strong emotions. Only one suicide left a note; and the fact that many of the suicides were drunk, used easily available methods which required little planning and were associated with marital discord and violence also suggested impulsiveness. Levy found no seasonal variation in the suicide rate.

Levy noted that suicide was condemned by the Navajo, but there is no belief in rewards and punishments after death. However, the ghosts of suicides do cause a little more trouble for the living than the ghosts of those dying natural deaths. The soul of a suicide does not leave the body easily and may make people who come into contact with it sick or suffer misfortune. Suicide is bad because it may harm others. However, the desire to harm others is rarely given as a motive for suicide, but Levy felt that it might be an unconscious motive behind some suicides.

With regard to acculturation stress, Levy felt that this was worse for young males, who are also less well integrated into domestic networks. The traditional male activities of raiding, hunting and warfare are no longer permitted, thereby eliminating some outlets for their frustration. The high incidence of alcohol use and abuse may be a result of this. It alleviates anxiety, overcomes social shyness and produces euphoria and oblivion. Levy felt that it contributed to the occurrence of suicidal behavior too.

Levy, et al. (1969) reported that 22% of Navajo murderers committed suicide after the act (much higher than, for example, Wolfgang [1958] found for murderers in Philadelphia). Those murderers committing suicide after the murder were all men, with a median age of 38, killing relatives, quite similar in characteristics to the other Navajo murderers.

Miller and Shoenfield (1971) studied the 54 Navajo who had attempted or completed suicide in a seven and a half month period in 1968-1969. This sample was primarily female, with a mean age of 22.8 for the women and 24.8 for the men. The modal suicidal person used drug ingestion, was from a modern background, was motivated by revenge or anger after a quarrel with a relative or romantic attachment, communicated their actions to others and had a diagnosis of depressive neurosis or adolescent adjustment reaction. The men and women did not differ in marital status or whether they came from a modern or traditional background. The men were more often intoxicated at the time of their suicidal act. The completed suicide rate can be calculated as roughly 13 per 100,000 per year.

OJIBWAY

Westermeyer and Brantner (1972) reported a suicide rate of 6.1 per 100,000 per year for the Ojibway on reservations in Northern Minnesota for 1940-1964 as compared to 10.7 for non-Indians.

Spaulding (1985-1986) calculated suicide rate for ten Ojibway Indian bands living in Northwestern Ontario for 1975-1982. The suicide rate for the Ojibway was 61.7, for all Ontario Indians and Eskimos 24.6 and for all Canadian Indians and Eskimos 36.3. Thus, the rate for these Ojibway bands was very high. The majority of the suicides were male, with a mean age of 30. The most popular methods for suicide were firearms followed by overdoses. Alcohol intoxication was common, and most of the suicides occurred on the home reserve or in a neighboring area. The bands differed in the incidence of suicide (36% of the suicides came from a band which constituted only 13% of the Ojibway population, but rates calculated for the different bands would be based on so few numbers as to be quite unreliable).

Spaulding noted that Ritzenthaler (1953) found no suicides from 1931-1940 among Ojibway living in Wisconsin, but Spaulding suggests that these bands may not have been undergoing acculturation during that period.

Westermeyer (1971) asserted that the suicide rate for the Ojibway in Minnesota was lower than that of whites in the surrounding counties, but he does not give the exact rates.

PAPAGO

Conrad and Kahn (1974) calculated suicides rates for Papago Indians of 18 for 1967-1971 (zero for 1967-1968 and 30 for 1969-1971). The most common methods were firearms and hanging, and the majority of the suicides were alcohol abusers, intoxicated at the time of the suicide, unemployed living off the main reservation, and living with spouses, and the most common precipitant was an interpersonal problems with the spouse or a relative. From 1969-1971 there were also 34 suicide attempters identified, mostly women, using overdoses. Two-thirds lived on the reservation, one-third lived with a spouse, only 28% were unemployed and almost half were alcohol abusers.

PUEBLO

Blanchard, et al. (1976) presented the case of an adolescent suicide from a Pueblo village. Juan had been in several fights in his community, always after drinking, and had been sentenced by a tribal judge to a 30-day sentence in the county detention home. After his release, a case conference was convened involving participants from the juvenile justice system, the mental health system, the school and his family. It was decided that Juan might benefit from an off-reservation boarding school. This placement worked well, and Juan developed a good relationship with the counselors and the psychologist there. Whereas at home he had a reputation for being difficult, at the school he was viewed as responsible and cooperative. He visited home on weekends, and he managed to refrain from drinking. Efforts were made to strengthen his relationship with his maternal uncle (a traditional bond), but Juan's father remained uninvolved with Juan. He tried to obtain a summer job with the Neighborhood Youth Corps at the school and at the boarding school itself, but these efforts failed. He went home for the summer and committed suicide within a few days.

Psychological tests given to Juan for the initial case conference indicated that he saw himself as being bad and unworthy, and he saw the world as moralistic, punitive, condemning and controlling. He had strong internal conflicts and a high anxiety level, and this prevented him socializing (unless drunk) which in turn increased his feeling of alienation.

In discussing this case, Blanchard noted that the tribal ways were disintegrating under the influence of the mainstream culture. Juan had lost his roots, and his own family was disintegrating. He felt hopeless in a cultural no-man's land. Juan encountered the racism in his early schooling, and he had internalized the negative feelings toward American Indians of his Anglo teachers. He was further alienated by his father's abandonment of the family. This analysis is problematic because, apart from the father's behavior, none of these speculations were documented in the case history. Blanchard seems to be proposing a standard explanation for this adolescent's suicide without producing any supporting evidence from the case history.

Levy (1965) calculated the suicide rates of eight Pueblos for the period 1954-1962. The lowest suicide rates were in the more traditional Pueblos (San Felipe 0.0, Zuni 2.8, Acoma 5.0, Santo Domingo 6.4 and Jemez 8.3), 16.7 in Taos where there were acute internal conflicts and highest in the acculturated Pueblos (Laguna 16.9 and Isleta 22.2).

SHOSHONI/BANNOCK

Dizmang (1968) counted fifteen suicides from 1960-1967 among the Shoshoni-Bannock on the Fort Hall Reservation in Idaho, giving a suicide rate of 98 per 100,000 per year. Thirteen of the suicides were under 35, and seven were under the age of twenty.

Dizmang compared to suicides with a group of high school graduates from the same reservation. He found that the suicides had more arrests, mainly for alcohol intoxication. They had also experienced more deaths of significant others. (In this respect, the suicides resembled a group of still-living alcohol abusers of the same age.) The parents were often alcoholics, unemployed and unstable. When agencies intervened, it was often to send the adolescent away for residential treatment or to boarding school which, though getting the adolescent out of the conflicts at home, left him separated from his friends and community. Here is a typical case reported by Dizmang:

> "John was the second oldest of six children. His parents were divorced when he was eleven years old. Both parents have severe, chronic problems with excessive alcohol intake. The parents often

> fought in public and abandoned the children frequently while drinking in town. On at least one occasion it was known that the children subsisted two or three days in succession from food scavenged from garbage cans. When John was 13 the court placed him and his brothers and sisters with the paternal grandparents. When he was 15 he and his younger brother were sent to boarding school some distance from the reservation, but shortly after this they were returned to the custody of the father. The records indicate that the father was still frequently drunk, never worked and was in and out of jail for disorderly conduct. The father apparently showed little interest in the children, and one by one they were shuttled back and forth between the father and the natural mother. By this time the mother had been married and divorced a second time and was married to her third husband. She was drinking heavily, and John and his two younger sisters were constantly in trouble with the law. Several months prior to his suicide, his mother divorced her third husband, his grandmother died, and on the day of John's death his sister wrecked his new car. John was overheard to say to a friend just prior to his suicide, "What's the use?" At age 20, John killed himself by hanging. Six months later the sister who had wrecked the John's car the day of his suicide killed herself by hanging while a prisoner in jail." (pp. 3-4)

Dizmang noted that the formation of the reservation had caused some social problems. The community was made up of several small unrelated bands. The government forced them together in the reservation, but these disparate bands had never managed to form a sense of community. Members from different bands were often given adjoining lands, making friction even more likely. The members of the tribes found it hard to be self-sufficient, and so they became dependent upon the government, which undermined their self-esteem and led to the development of a self-defeating pattern of behavior. Attempts by the government to change these patterns were typically inconsistent and ineffective.

There was a great deal of mutual distrust and alienation between the American Indians and the local white communities. The American Indians disliked the whites so much that acculturation (becoming like a white man) was viewed with disapproval. This inhibited the American Indians with potential from succeeding in the white culture.

Dizmang suggested that suicide might be prevented by identifying the high risk adolescents and getting them help. This would require the cooperation of all of the local agencies and the recruitment of indigenous staff to work with the adolescents. Dizmang also urged that drunken belligerent American Indian adolescents be treated as medical problems rather than as criminal problems. They should be evaluated and followed-up aggressively by the mental health teams. If no stable home was possible, then residential half-way houses should be established, not far removed from the adolescent's community.

Dizmang, et al. (1974) continued their discussion of suicide in this community. In earlier days, the group split up into small bands of two to forty people who hunted, gathered and camped together. The groups were fluid, with people joining and leaving at will. The children were raised by the women as a group which protected the children from loss through death of a parent. Emotional self-sufficiency was stressed in the child-rearing, and children's needs were taken care of without the children having to ask. Aggression was permitted only against outside enemies.

The creation of the reservation in 1869 disrupted this life style. The land was parceled out to individuals in 1887 which broke up the extended families. They began to depend upon trade with whites and, as their source of food and shelter was decimated, the American Indians became even more dependent upon the whites. The skills of the male were now irrelevant, and his role within the culture and the family deprived of meaning.

Dizmang and his colleagues identified ten suicides under the age of 25 from 1961 to 1968 on the reservation. (There were seven older suicides during this same period.) For each suicide, four nonsuicidal controls were chosen matched for age, gender, and degree of Indian blood.

Several clear differences emerged. The suicides had more often been cared for by more than one significant caretaker and had more often experienced two or more losses through desertion or divorce, their caretakers had been arrested more often, they had been arrested more often in the prior 12 months and had been arrested for the first time at an earlier age (though the two groups did not differ in the total number of arrests), and they had more often attended boarding school.

After consultation from the National Institutes of Mental Health in 1967, the tribe was urged to set up a medical facility on the reservation for youths arrested for intoxication or disorderly behavior rather than placing them in the white jails. The facility was established and staffed by tribal volunteers, and no youth suicide had occurred in the first 18 month period studied.

Sioux

Curlee (1969) described suicidal behavior occurring among the Sioux on the Cheyenne River Reservation in South Dakota. In a recent year there had been 15 attempted suicides (though no deaths) which came to the attention of the hospital in a population of 3,700 people. Thirteen of the attempters were between the ages of 15 and 21, and the majority were girls. Curlee saw the distress in this tribe, as evidenced by the high rate of attempted suicide, as a result of partial acculturation. The youths had adopted some, but not all, of the mainstream values and these conflicted with the traditional values. The youths were unable to model themselves on their parents since their parents had not faced such a clear conflict. There was low self-esteem and little pride in being an Indian. In the youth, this led to suicide, in the older adults alcoholism and violence.

The Sioux permit their children a great deal of autonomy about matters such as education and health, but the children often become quite spoilt, accustomed to having their own way. Many of the suicide attempts were seen by Curlee as efforts to manipulate others so that they would get what they wanted.

Mindell and Stuart (1969) reported on suicide attempts among the Sioux [Oglala] on the Pine Ridge Indian Reservation in South Dakota. In one year, they recorded 21 suicide attempts and five serious suicidal threats. The modal attempter was a woman under the age of 29, single and of mixed blood. The attempt was relatively nonlethal, probably by means of an overdose. About a third of the attempters had contacted the reservation hospital in the previous week to see a physician. The most common psychiatric diagnosis was neurosis. The attempt was typically precipitated by rejection from a significant other who was involved with the attempter in an intense, hostile-dependent or symbiotic relationship.

They presented the case of a suicide attempt in an 18 year-old girl. Mary was the oldest child, with a younger brother aged 13, living with their parents. When she was 14, Mary ran away from the boarding school and, despite being jailed for truancy, refused to return. Her mother let her stay home, a decision consistent with the trend to grant children a great deal of autonomy. She was very close to an aunt with whom she would discuss her problems. This aunt died in July, 1966, quite suddenly. Mary was very upset and refused to go to church anymore. She began to think about dying so that she could rejoin her aunt. In August, she cut her wrists. She felt that her mother favored the younger brother and that her father was particularly interested in her. On the night of her suicide attempt, Mary complained to her mother about some noisy relatives who had visited, and her mother "bawled [Mary] out" (p. 26). Mary then took an overdose of Phenobarbital and went to bed. When she awoke in the morning, her mother took her to the hospital.

In analyzing this case, Mindell and Stuart saw the suicide attempt as a defense against her murderous wishes toward her mother. The attempt forces her mother to care for Mary and serves to maintain a relationship with her mother. Interestingly, the result of a psychological analysis of the case minimizes the role of socio-cultural and socio-political factors. The oppression of American Indians does not appear in Mindell and Stuart's analysis.

Claymore (1988) reported that the age-adjusted suicide rate among the Sioux in the Aberdeen area in South Dakota in 1981-1983 was 30.9 as compared to 11.6 for the USA as a whole. However, on one reservation the age-adjusted suicide rate for this period was 70.3. The crude rate was 66, though this dropped to 53.4 in 1986. In 1986, the official attempted suicide rate was 1281 per 100,000 per year.

From October 1985 though September 1986, there were three completed suicides and 72 suicide attempts on this reservation. All the teenage males used hanging, whereas males over the age of twenty and all females preferred overdoses. Thirty-nine of the individuals had a history of attempted suicide, 64% were intoxicated with alcohol at the time of the suicidal act, 39% had contact with mental health staff and 33% had chronic medical problems. The suicides peaked on Wednesdays and in December and April/May. Weather conditions were not related to the incidence of suicidal behavior.

May (undated) examined suicidal behavior among the Sioux [Oglala] on the Pine Ridge Reservation for one year (mainly 1971). The mental health staff arranged for a staff member to be called for every suicide attempter presenting at the health facilities, and they collected information on a standardized form. In the year studied, there were eight completed suicides, giving a suicide rate of 72.7. The modal suicide was young (median age 20), single, of mixed blood and equally often male and female. They used medication, committed suicide at home (or near their home), after drinking.

One hundred and four suicide attempts were registered, giving a rate of 945. The modal suicide attempter was female, median age 21 (the median age for men was 28 and for women 20), single, of full blood and occurring in October. Some of the regions in the reservation had higher rates than others, and the attempters appeared to come from more fragmented families (fewer extended households and more divorced and separated parents). Thirty percent of the attempters were students, and 42% of the rest were unemployed, the same as for the reservation in general. Thirty-nine percent had previously attempted suicide. The most common method was overdose, generally at home, and half had been drinking at the time. The most common precipitant was an argument or fight with a family member, and the mental health staff thought that the most common reason was to change an important relationship in some way.

Other Groups

Sievers, et al. (1975) studied completed and attempted suicides in the Phoenix Indian Health Service region for 1971 to June, 1972. The estimated suicide rates were 40 for the Apache and 7 for the Pima (with rates of 932 and 764 for attempted suicide respectively). The women more often attempted suicide, used drug overdoses more often and died less often. Eight percent of the completed suicides and 18% of the attempted suicides used Isoniazid (a medication used for the treatment of tuberculosis), and Sievers claimed (without documentation) that the frequency of prescription of this medication for each of the many tribes paralleled the use of the drug for suicidal behavior.

Sievers, et al., (1990) looked at mortality records for Pima/Papago Indians who had lived on a reservation between 1975 and 1984, and calculated a suicide rate of 53 for them (compared to the official suicide rate of 49).

Kraus and Buffler (1979) calculated rates in Alaska for 1971-1977 of roughly [Athabascan] 80, [Northwest] Eskimo 70, Tlingit 30, [Southwest] Eskimo 20 and Aleut 10. (The rates had to be read off of a figure provided by the authors in their paper.) Kost-Grant (1983) calculated suicides rates in Alaska for 1978-1980 of 28.3 for Eskimos, 21.4 for American Indians and 28.9 for Aleuts. In British Columbia from 1973-1982, Hochkirchen and Jilek (1985b) reported a suicide rate of 100 for two small coastal communities where more than 90% of the people spoke Kwakiutl, and 19.4 for an inland region where about 60% spoke the Tsimshian language. (Suicide was more common among the adolescents and young adults in these communities, but equally split between men and women.)

Mahoney, et al. (1989) studied the Seneca from 1955-1984 and found higher standard mortality ratios for suicidal deaths for both men and women, but not significantly so. Focusing on those aged 0-24, Michalek found a high standard mortality ratio for males but not for females.

CONCLUSIONS

This review of research on suicidal behavior in different American Indian tribes has made it clear that suicide rates do vary tremendously from tribe to tribe, and we will return to this issue in the next chapter.

The review has also revealed that most commentators believe that the oppressed status of American Indians and the clash of modern American culture with traditional American Indian culture are both important contributors to the causation of American Indian suicide. However, it is noteworthy that the data presented by these commentators are largely irrelevant to these hypotheses. The research reveals motives for suicidal behavior, for example, that are found in other ethnic groups, such as marital conflict.

No researcher has yet devised a measure of culture conflict or of acculturation which could be given to samples of American Indians so that the scores of suicidal and nonsuicidal tribal members could be compared. The discussions of suicidal behavior in American Indians are not data based, but rather rely on the opinions of the writer. This is true, for example, of the discussions by Levy and his colleagues and by Blanchard, to name just two.

It is crucial in future research on American Indian suicide that we move from informed opinions to documented research. If culture clash, anomie, alienation and related variables play a role in American suicidal behavior, then measures of these variables must be devised (and some already exist -- for example, there are good psychological tests of anomie and alienation), and their role in predicting suicidal behavior in American Indians explored.

REFERENCES

Anon. Suicide among the Blackfoot Indians. *Bulletin of Suicidology*, 1970, #7, 42-43.

Bartell, G. D. Apache suicide patterns. 36th International Congress of Americanists, Spain, 1964, unpublished.

Barter, J. T., & Weist, K. M. Historical and contemporary patterns of Northern Cheyenne suicide. Sacramento Medical Center, California, 1970.

Blanchard, J. D., Blanchard, E. L., & Roll, S. A psychological autopsy of an Indian adolescent suicide with implications for community services. *Suicide & Life-Threatening Behavior*, 1976, 6, 3-10.

Claymore, B. J. A public health approach to suicide attempts on a Sioux reservation. *American Indian & Alaska Native Mental Health Research*, 1988, 1(3), 19-24.

Conrad, R. D., & Kahn, M. An epidemiological study of suicide among the Papago Indians. *American Journal of Psychiatry*, 1974, 131, 69-72.

Curlee, W. V. Suicide and self-destructive behavior on the Cheyenne River Reservation. In *Suicide among American Indians*. Washington, DC: US Department of Health, Education, & Welfare, 1969, 34-36. PHS Publication No. 1903.

Devereux, G. Primitive psychiatry. *Bulletin of the History of Medicine*, 1942, 11, 522-542.

Dizmang, L. H. Suicide among the Cheyenne Indians. *Bulletin of Suicidology*, 1967, #1, 8-11.

Dizmang, L. H. Observations on suicidal behavior among the Shoshone-Bannock Indians. Paper presented at the American Association of Suicidology conference, Chicago, 1968.

Dizmang, L. H., Watson, J., May, P. A., & Bopp, J. Adolescent suicide at an Indian reservation. *American Journal of Orthopsychiatry*, 1974, 44, 43-49.

Durkheim, E. *Le suicide*. Paris: Felix Alcan, 1897.

Everett, M. W. Pathology in White Mountain Apache culture. *Western Canadian Journal of Anthropology*, 1970, 2, 180-203.

Everett, M. W., Baha, C. J., Decaly, E., Endfield, M. R., & Selby, K. Parents, children, and friends. University of Kentucky, undated.

Foulks, E. F. Psychological continuities. *Journal of Operational Psychiatry*, 1980, 11(2), 156-161.

Hochkirchen, B., & Jilek, W. Psychosocial dimensions of suicide and parasuicide in Amerindians of the Pacific Northwest. *Journal of Operational Psychiatry*, 1985a, 16(2), 24-28.

Hochkirchen, B. H., & Jilek, W. G. Psychodynamics of self-destructive behavior in Native Americans. In P. Pichot, P. Berner, R. Wolf & K. Thau (Eds.) *Psychiatry: The state of the art, Volume 8*. New York: Plenum, 1985b, 519-525.

Hrdlicka, A. *Physiological and medical observations among the Indians of southwestern United States and northern Mexico*. Washington, DC: Bureau of American Ethnology, Bulletin #34, 1908.

Humphrey, J. A., & Kupferer, H. J. Homicide and suicide among the Cherokee and Lumbee Indians of North Carolina. *International Journal of Social Psychiatry*, 1982, 28, 121-128.

Kost-Grant, B. L. Self-inflicted gunshot wounds among Alaska Natives. *Public Health Reports*, 1983, 98, 72-78.

Kraus, R. F., & Buffler, P. A. Sociocultural stress and the American Native in Alaska. *Culture, Medicine & Psychiatry*, 1979, 3, 111-151.

Kupferer, H. J., & Humphrey, J. A. Fatal Indian violence in North Carolina. *Anthropological Quarterly*, 1975, 48, 236-244.

Leighton, A. H., & Hughes, C. C. Notes on Eskimo patterns of suicide. *Southwestern Journal of Anthropology*, 1955, 11, 327-338.

Levy, J. E. Navajo suicide. *Human Organization*, 1965, 24, 308-318.

Levy, J. E., & Kunitz, S. J. Notes on some White Mountain Apache social pathologies. *Plateau*, 1969, 42, 11-19.

Levy, J. E., & Kunitz, S. J. Indian reservations, anomie, and social disorganization. *Southwestern Journal of Anthropology*, 1971, 27(2), 97-128.

Levy, J. E., & Kunitz, S. J. A suicide prevention program for Hopi youth. *Social Science & Medicine*, 1987, 25, 931-940.

Levy, J. E., Kunitz, S. J., & Everett, M. W. Navajo criminal homicide. *Southwestern Journal of Anthropology*, 1969, 25(2), 124-152.

Mahoney, M. C., Michalek, A. M., Cummings, K. M., Nasca, P. C., & Emrich, L. J. Mortality in a northeastern Native American cohort. *American Journal of Epidemiology*, 1989, 129, 816-826

May, P. A. Suicide and suicide attempts on the Pine Ridge Reservation. Undated.

Michalek, A. M., Mahoney, M. C., Buck, G., & Snyder, R. Mortality patterns among the youth of a northeastern American Indian cohort. *Public Health Reports*, 1993, 108, 403-407.

Miller, S. I., & Shoenfield, L. S. Suicide attempt patterns among the Navaho Indians. *International Journal of Social Psychiatry*, 1971, 17, 189-193.

Mindell, C., & Stuart, P. Suicide and self-destructive behavior in the Oglala Sioux. In *Suicide among American Indians*. Washington, DC: US Department of Health, Education, & Welfare, 1969, 25-33. PHS Publication No. 1903.

Ritzenthaler, R. E. Chippewa preoccupation with health. *Bulletin of the Public Museum of the City of Milwaukee*, 1953, 19(4), 175-258.

Sievers, M. L., Cynamon, M. H., & Bittker, T. E. Intentional Isoniazid overdosage among southwestern American Indians. *American Journal of Psychiatry*, 1975, 132, 662-665.

Sievers, M. L., Nelson, R. G., & Bennett, P. H. Adverse mortality experience of a southwestern American Indian community. *Journal of Clinical Epidemiology*, 1990, 43, 1231-1242.

Simpson, S. G., Reid, R., Baker, S. P., & Teret, S. Injuries among the Hopi Indians. *Journal of the American Medical Association*, 1983, 249, 1873-1876.

Spaulding, J. M. Recent suicide rates among ten Ojibwa Indian bands in Northwestern Ontario. *Omega*, 1985-1986, 16, 347-354.

Thurman, P. J., Martin, D., & Martin, M. An assessment of attempted suicides among adolescent Cherokee Indians. *Journal of Non-White Concerns in Personnel and Guidance*, 1985, 13, 176-182.

Westermeyer, J. Disorganization. *American Journal of Psychiatry*, 1971, 128, 123.

Westermeyer, J., & Brantner, J. Violent death and alcohol use. *Minnesota Medicine*, 1972, 55, 749-752.

Wolfgang, M. E. *Patterns of criminal homicide*. Philadelphia: University of Pennsylvania Press, 1958.

Wyman, L. C., & Thorne, B. Notes on Navaho suicide. *American Anthropologist*, 1945, 47, 278-288.

Chapter 8

SUICIDE RATES BY TRIBE: A SUMMARY

The problem addressed in the present chapter is the identification of which American Indian tribes have high suicide rates. We have reviewed studies on American Indian suicide rates in this book, and this chapter collects together all of the reported suicide rates. Three other investigators have provided similar tables, and their compilations of suicide rates are also reported here. Then these two sets of suicide rates are summarized in a final table. Only suicide rates for specified tribes (rather than regions and mixed groups of American Indians) will be noted.

The rates reported by others are shown in Table 1. The rates identified by the present author and discussed in this book are shown in Table 2. These rates are combined (together with corrections) and presented in Table 3.

The American Indian tribes with low estimated suicide rates are the Navajo, Pueblo (Hopi) and the Ojibway in the 1960's and the Aleut, Lumbee and Pima in the 1970's. The American Indian tribes with high estimated suicide rates are the Blackfoot, Papago, and Shoshoni in the 1960's and the Kwakiutl, Shoshoni and Sioux in the 1970's.

Table 1 Summary of Suicide Rates for American Indian tribes

Tribe	years	suicide rate	source	summary source*
Apache	1957-1959	43	Van Winkle/May, 1986	Anon, 1989
(White Mountain)	1924-1971	33	Everett, 1975	M&S, 1980-1981
(White Mountain)	1930-1970	50	Webb/Willard, 1975	M&S, 1980-1981
(White Mountain)	1965-1967	20	Levy/Kunitz, 1969	M, 1983-1984
[San Carlos]	1958-1968	37	Everett, 1975	M&S, 1980-1981
[Arizona]	1971-1973	40	Sievers, et al., 1975	M&S, 1980-1981
[New Mexico]	1953-1962	21	Levy, 1965	M&S, 1980-1981
Blackfoot	1960's	130	Anon, 1970	Anon, 1989
Cherokee	1973	23	Kupferer/Humphrey, 1975	M, 1983-1984
Cherokee	1972-1973	12	Humphrey/Kupferer, 1982	M&V, 1994
	1974-1976	31		
Cherokee	1981-1982	0	Thurman, et, 1985	M&V, 1994
Cheyenne [Northern]	1960-1968	48	Barter/Weist (in Shore, 1975)	M&S, 1980-1981
Lumbee	1972	4	Peck in Kupferer/ Humphrey, 1975	M, 1983-1984
	1973	13	Peck in Kupferer/ Humphrey, 1975	M, 1983-1984
Lumbee	1972-1973	8	Humphrey/Kupferer, 1982	M&V, 1994
	1974-1976	10		
Navajo	1954-1963	10	Levy, 1965	Anon, 1989
Navajo	1954-1963	8	Levy, 1965	M&S, 1980-1981
Navajo	?	10	Havighurst,	
Navajo	1968-1969	13	Miller, 1971#	Anon, 1989
Navajo	1968-1969	13	Miller/Schoenfeld, 1971	M&S, 1980-1981
Ojibway	1940-1969	6	Westermeyer, 1972	Anon, 1989

Table 1 Summary of Suicide Rates for American Indian tribes (continued)

Tribe	years	suicide rate	source	summary source*
Ojibway [Minnesota]	1940-1964	6	Westermeyer/Brantner, 1972	M, 1983-1984
Ojibway	1975-1982	62	Spaulding, 1985-1986	M&V, 1994
Ojibway	1971-1974	23	Fox, et, 1984	M&V, 1994
	1975	267		
	1976-1980	28		
Papago	1960-1970	100	Conrad, 1972	Anon, 1989
Papago	1969-1971	30	Conrad/Kahn, 1973/1974	M&S, 1980-1981
Papago	1967-1971	18	Conrad/Kahn, 1973/1974	M&S, 1980-1981
Pima [Arizona]	1960-1970s	40	Sievers, et, 1975	Anon, 1989
Pueblo [New Mexico]	1953-1962	10	Levy, 1965	M&S, 1980-1981
Pueblo	1960-1962	45	Biernoff, 1969	M&V, 1994
	1963-1965	46		
	1966-1968	74		
Pueblo (Hopi)	1965-1969	8	Levy/Kunitz, 1971	M&S, 1980-1981
	1956-1965	12	Levy/Kunitz, 1982	M&V, 1994
	1961-1970	28		
	1966-1975	29		
	1971-1979	39		
Shoshone	1972-1976	38	Berman, 1979	M&V, 1994
Shoshoni-Arapaho	1980's	50	Bechtold, 1988	M&V, 1994
Shoshoni-Arapaho	1985	230	Tower, 1989	M&V, 1994
Shoshoni-Bannock	1890-1972	39	Levy, et, 1972	M, 1983-1984
	1890-1939	20		
	1940-1969	49		
	1940-1949	34		

Table 1 Summary of Suicide Rates for American Indian tribes (continued)

Tribe	years	suicide rate	source	summary source*
Shoshoni-Bannock (continued)				
	1950-1959	38		
	1960-1969	76		
	1970-1972	167		
Shoshoni-Bannock	1960's	100	Watson, 1969	Anon, 1989
Shoshoni-Bannock	1960-1967	98	Dizmang, 1968	Anon, 1989
Shoshoni-Bannock	1961-1968	98	Dizmang, et, 1974	M&S, 1980-1981
Shoshoni-Bannock	1960-1966	83	Havighurst, 1971	M&S, 1980-1981
Shoshoni-Bannock	1960-1969	69	Havighurst, 1971	M&S, 1980-1981
Shoshoni-Paiute	1938-1970	100	Duck Valley, 1970	Anon, 1989
Shoshoni-Paiute	1949-1978	117	Berman, 1979	M, 1983-1984
	1969-1978	150		
Sioux	1971-1973	73	May, 1973	M&V, 1994
Sioux	1981-1983	66	Claymore, 1988	M&V, 1994
Yaqui	1969-1971	30	Conrad/Kahn, 1974	Anon, 1989

This reference is probably incorrectly given in Anon (1989). It should be Miller and Schoenfeld (1971).

* The sources are:

M&S McIntosh and Santos (1980-1981)
M McIntosh (1983-1984)
M&V May and van Winkle (1994)
Anon Anon (1989)

Table 2. Suicide rates of American Indian tribes identified in the present book

tribe	*years*	*suicide rate*
Aleut	1971-1977	10
Aleut	1978-1980	28.9
Apache	1971-1972	40
Apache (Mescalero/Jicarilla)	1954-1963	20.8
Apache (White Mountain)	1965-1967	20
[Athabascan]	1971-1977	81
Blackfoot	1960's	125
Cherokee	1972-1973	11.5
	1974-1976	31.1
Cheyenne	1910's	22
	1920's	21
	1930's	13
	1940's	6
	1950's	40
	1960-1968	48
Eskimo	1978-1980	28.3
Eskimo [northwest]	1971-1877	70
Eskimo [southwest]	1971-1977	20
Kwakiutl	1963-1972	50/31
	1973-1982	175/123
Lumbee	1972-1973	8.3
	1974-1976	10.3
Navajo	1961	16.1
	1962	9
	1954-1963	8.3
	1968-1969	13
Ojibway	1940-1964	6.1
	1975-1982	61.7

Table 2 (Continued)

Papago	1967-1971	18
Pima	1971-1972	7
Pima/Papago	1975-1984	49-53
Pueblo	1954-1963	10.2
	1954-1962#	0
		2.8
		5.0
		6.4
		8.3
		16.3
		16.9
		22.2
Pueblo (Hopi)	1956-1965	8
	1961-1970	13
	1966-1975	14-30
	1971-1980	25-35
	1981	24*
	1982	23*
	1983	14*
	1984	13*
	1985	13*
	1979-1980	27
Shoshoni-Bannock	1960-1967	98
Sioux	1971	72.2
	1981-1983	30.9
Tlingit	1971-1977	30

for different Pueblo groups
* three-year moving-average

Table 3. Tribal suicide rates in America: A Summary

tribe	1910's	1920's	1930's	1940's	1950's	1960's	1970's	1980's
Aleut							16	
Apache					26	18	40	
Blackfoot						125		
Cherokee							23	
Cheyenne	22	21	13	6	40	48		
Eskimo							42	
Kwakiutl						40	149	
Lumbee							9	
Navajo					8	13		
Ojibway				←	6	→	56	
Papago						100		
Pima						40	7	
Pueblo					10	55		
Pueblo (Hopi)					8	13	30	17
Shoshoni							38	
Shoshoni-Bannock					98			
Shoshoni-Paiute			←	—	113	—	→	
Sioux							73	31
Tlingit							30	
Yaqui						30		

Ratings Made by Anthropologists for Earlier Times

Several anthropologists have rated the incidence of suicide in primitive societies, including some North American groups. In this section, we will examine the data which these studies provide.

Masumura (1977) rated 35 nations for the frequency of suicide, eight of which were American Indian societies, by having judges read the suicide entries in the Human Relations Area Files, and his ratings are shown below.

In parentheses after each score provided by the original investigator(s), I have indicated z-scores based solely on the North American societies.

Group	suicide score (range 2-8)
Creek	6 (+0.48)
Crow	6 (+0.48)
Iroquois	5 (0.00)
Kwakiutl	8 (+1.45)
Navajo	2 (-1.45)
Ojibway	7 (+0.97)
Omaha	4 (-0.48)
Pomo	2 (-1.45)

From this group, it would appear that the Kwakiutl have a relatively high suicide rate and the Pomo a relatively low suicide rate.

Palmer (1965) rated forty societies for their suicide rates, eleven of which were American Indian societies, also by reading the suicide entries in the Human Relations Area Files. The scores for these eleven societies were:

Group	suicide score (range 0-21)
Ahtena	6 (-0.14)
Comanche	21 (+2.21)
Kwakiutl	6 (-0.14)
Nahane (Kaska)	2 (-0.77)
Navajo	8 (+0.17)
Omaha	2 (-0.77)
Papago	2 (-0.77)
Pueblo (Hopi)	18 (+1.74)
Pueblo [Taos]	6 (-0.14)
Pueblo (Zuni)	0 (-1.08)
Sanpoil	5 (-0.30)

Among this group, the Comanche and Hopi appear to have relatively high suicide rates while the Zuni appear to have a relatively low suicide rate.

Krauss (1970) counted the number of detailed cases of suicide in 58 societies, ten of which were American Indian societies. This same sample of societies was scored by Naroll (1963) using an index based on the amount of wordage about suicide. These two measures were both then used as proxy measures of the suicide rate. The scores were:

Group	Krauss score	Naroll score
	(range 0-84)	(range 34-74)
Ahtena	2 (-0.45)	45 (-0.82)
Apache (White Mountain)	3 (-0.31)	57 (+0.29)
Cheyenne	9 (+0.54)	65 (+1.02)
Clallam	1 (-0.59)	50 (-0.36)
Eyak	0 (-0.73)	52 (-0.18)
Iroquois	25 (+2.79)	74 (+1.85)
Ojibway	5 (-0.03)	55 (+0.10)
Paiute, Southern	0 (-0.73)	34 (-1.83)
Papago	2 (-0.45)	45 (-0.82)
Wintun	5 (-0.03)	62 (+0.75)

From Krauss's scores, it appears that the Iroquois have a relatively high rate of suicide; from Naroll's scores it appears that the Iroquois and Cheyenne have a relatively high suicide rate while the Southern Paiute have a relatively low suicide rate.

Naroll (1962) estimated rates of "protest" suicide which he defined as voluntary suicide committed in such a way as to come to public attention (a category which excluded suicide to avoid capital punishment, suicides designated by custom as in suttee, and those not consciously intended). His rates for the Native American cultures were: (1) Iroquois (Seneca; 1855-

1936) 6.48 per 100,000 per year, (2) Navajo (San Juan County; 1900-1942) 5.15, and (3) Paiute (Harney Valley; 1856-1935) 117.

There were several vague reports from which Naroll could not estimate rates, but he judged that the Aleut and Sanpoil seemed to have a high suicide rate while the Ahtena seemed to have a low rate.

In his study of the aged in primitive societies, Simmons (1945) rated suicide in the elderly in only four Native American societies for men and only two of these for women.[8] The codings for the men (on a scale of 0 to 3) were:

Crow	2 (both men and women)
Eskimo [Polar]	3 (both men and women)
Ojibway	1 (men only)
Omaha	1 (men only)

Thus, the Eskimo [Polar] appear to have a high incidence of suicide among the elderly.

In the most comprehensive set of ratings yet, Ember and Ember (1992) had judges rate 186 societies for their suicide rate based on data in the Human Relations Area Files, including 30 North American tribes. Ratings were possible for 19 of these 30 tribes. Ember and Ember have drawn attention to the fact that the materials on suicides in the Human Relations Area Files come from very different time periods. Therefore, they specified the year from which the data were derived.

The ratings made by the Embers do not permit grossly deviant z-scores, but it appears that the Huron had a relatively high suicide rate from anthropological reports made in 1634.

[8] Simmons adds the words "willingness to die" next to the label "Suicide," causing doubt as to what he was actually coding.

Group	Suicide	Score	Year
Ahtena	1.25	(-0.43)	1915
Aleut	2	(+0.91)	1778
Bella Coola	1	(-0.87)	1880
Comanche	2	(+0.91)	1870
Creek	1.75	(+0.46)	1800
Eyak	2	(+0.91)	1890
Gros Ventre	2	(+0.91)	1880
Hidatsa	1.75	(+0.46)	1836
Huron	3	(+2.70)	1634
Ingalik	1.5	(+0.02)	1885
Klamath	1	(-0.87)	1860
Micmac	1	(-0.87)	1650
Montagnais-Naskapi (Montagnais)	1	(-0.87)	1910
Nahane (Kaska)	1	(-0.87)	1900
Omaha	1	(-0.87)	1860
Papago	1	(-0.87)	1910
Pawnee	2	(+0.91)	1867
Pomo [East Pomo]	1	(-0.87)	1850
Pueblo (Zuni)	1	(-0.87)	1880

Summary

From these ratings, the Cheyenne, Comanche, Eskimo [Polar], Huron, Iroquois, Kwakiutl, Paiute and Pueblo (Hopi) have a relatively high estimated suicide rate while the Pomo, Southern Paiute and Zuni have a relatively low estimated suicide rate. There is one inconsistency here, with different investigators arriving at different estimates for the Paiute.

Conclusions

It is interesting to observe that anthropologists have written about suicidal behavior in the past in societies which have often not been studied much at all today by modern epidemiologists, such as the Huron, Iroquois, Pomo and Zuni. Thus, it is difficult to compare the estimated suicide rates in American Indian tribes in the past and in recent times.

However, the two sets of estimates agree that suicide is common among the Kwakiutl, and disagree about the Pueblo (Hopi). Thus, the Kwakiutl may have a long history of frequent suicidal behavior, while the Pueblo (Hopi) may have recently experienced an increase in suicidal behavior.

These comparisons indicate that it would of great interest were epidemiologists to undertake investigations of mortality in more American Indian tribes, especially those studied by anthropologists, such as American Indian tribes in the northeast section of America. It would also be of interest were the Human Relations Area Files to incorporate reports from more American Indian tribes into their sample so that tribes which have studied by epidemiologists in recent years can be examined for their suicidal behavior in the past.

References

Anon. Suicide among the Blackfoot Indians. *Bulletin of Suicidology*, 1970, #7, 42-43.

Anon. *Suicide and ethnicity in the United States*. New York: Brunner/Mazel, 1989.

Bechtold, D. W. Cluster suicide in American Indian adolescents. *American Indian & Alaska Native Mental Health Research*, 1988, 1(3), 26-35.

Berman, A. L. A socio-cultural autopsy. American Association of Suicidology, Denver, 1979.

Berman, A. L. Suicide on the Duck Valley Indian Reservation. Final Report, 1979.

Biernoff, M. A report on Pueblo Indian suicide. Unpublished, 1969.

Claymore, B. J. A public health approach to suicide attempts on a Sioux reservation. *American Indian & Alaska Native Mental Health Research*, 1988, 1(3), 119-24.

Conrad, R. D. Suicide among the Papago Indians. MA thesis, University of Arizona, 1972.

Conrad, R. D., & Kahn, M. W. An epidemiological study of suicide and suicide attempts among the Papago Indians. *Proceedings of the 81st. Annual Conference of the American Psychological Association*, 1973, 8, part 1, 449-450.

Conrad, R. D., & Kahn, M. W. An epidemiological study of suicide among the Papago Indians. *American Journal of Psychiatry*, 1974, 131, 69-72.

Dizmang, L. H. Observations on suicidal behavior among the Shoshone-Bannock Indians. First Annual National Conference on Suicidology, Chicago, 1968.

Dizmang, L. H., Watson, J., May, P. A., & Bopp, J. Adolescent suicide at an Indian reservation. *American Journal of Orthopsychiatry*, 1974, 44, 43-49.

Duck Valley. *Suicide among the Shoshone-Paiute on the Duck Valley Reservation.* Owyee, NV: Duck Valley Indian Reservation Tribal Mental Health Committee, 1970.

Ember, C. R., & Ember, R. Warfare, aggression, and resource problems. *Behavior Science Research*, 1992, 26, 169-226.

Everett, M. W. American Indian "social pathology." In T. R. Williams (Ed.) *Psychological anthropology*. Paris: Mouton, 1975, 249-285.

Fox, J., Manitonabi, D., & Ward, J. A. An Indian community with a high suicide rate. *Canadian Journal of Psychiatry*, 1984, 29, 425-427.

Havighurst, R. J. The extent and significance of suicide among American Indians today. *Mental Hygiene*, 1971, 55, 174-177.

Humphrey, J. A., & Kupferer, H. J. Homicide and suicide among the Cherokee and Lumbee Indians of North Carolina. *International Journal of Social Psychiatry*, 1982, 28(2), 121-128.

Krauss, H. H. Social development and suicide. *Journal of Cross-Cultural Psychology*, 1970, 1, 159-167.

Kupferer, H. J., & Humphrey, J. A. Fatal Indian violence in North Carolina. *Anthropological Quarterly*, 1975, 48, 236-244.

Levy, J. E. Navajo suicide. *Human Organization*, 1965, 24, 308-318.

Levy, J. E., & Kunitz, S. J. Notes on some White Mountain Apache social pathologies. *Plateau*, 1969, 42, 11-19.

Levy, J. E., & Kunitz, S. J. Indian reservations, anomie, and social pathologies. *Southwestern Journal of Anthropology*, 1971, 27, 97-128.

Levy, J. E., & Kunitz, S. J. A suicide prevention program for Hopi youth. *Social Science & Medicine*, 1987, 25, 930-940.

Levy, J. E., Shore, J. H., & Gordon, D. Suicide prevention among Shoshone-Bannock Indians. Final Report, NIMH Grant MH-18984-01, 1972.

Masumura, W. T. Social integration and suicide. *Behavior Science Research*, 1977, 12, 251-269.

May, P. A. Suicide and suicide attempts on the Pine Ridge Reservation. Unpublished, 1973.

May, P. A., & Van Winkle, N. W. Durkheim's suicide theory and its applicability to contemporary American Indians and Alaska Natives. In D. Lester (Ed.) *Emile Durkheim: Le Suicide 100 hundred years later*. Philadelphia: Charles Press, 1994, 296-318.

McIntosh, J. L. Suicide among Native Americans. *Omega*, 1983-1984, 14, 215-229.

McIntosh, J. L., & Santos, J. F. Suicide among Native Americans. *Omega*, 1980-1981, 11, 303-316.

Miller, M. Suicides on a southwestern American Indian reservation. *White Cloud Journal*, 1971, 1(3), 14-18.

Miller, S. I., & Schoenfeld, L. S. Suicide attempt patterns among the Navajo Indians. *International Journal of Social Psychiatry*, 1971, 17, 189-193.

Naroll, R. *Data quality control*. New York: Free Press, 1962.

Naroll, R. Thwarting disorientation and suicide. Unpublished manuscript. Evanston, IL: Northwestern University, 1963.

Palmer, S. Murder and suicide in forty nonliterate societies. *Journal of Criminal Law, Criminology & Police Science*, 1965, 56, 320-324.

Shore, J. H. Suicide and suicide attempts among American Indians of the Pacific Northwest. *International Journal of Social Psychiatry*, 1972, 18, 91-96.

Sievers, M., Cynamon, M., & Bittker, T. Intentional Isoniazid overdosage among southwestern American Indians. *American Journal of Psychiatry*, 1975, 132, 662-665.

Simmons, L. W. *The role of the aged in primitive society*. New Haven: Yale University Press, 1945.

Spaulding, J. M. Recent suicide rates among ten Ojibwa Indian bands in northwestern Ontario. *Omega*, 1985-1986, 16, 347-354.

Thurman, P. J., Martin, D., & Martin, M. An assessment of attempted suicides among adolescent Cherokee Indians. *Journal of Multicultural Counseling & Development*, 1985, 13(4), 176-182.

Tower, M. A suicide epidemic in an American Indian community. *American Indian & Alaska Native Mental Health Research*, 1989, 3(1), 34-44.

Van Winkle, N., & May, P. A. Native American suicide in New Mexico, 1957-1979. *Human Organization*, 1986, 45, 296-309.

Watson, J. *The etiology of suicide at Fort Hall*. Subcommittee of Indian Education, Volume 5. Washington, DC: US Government Printing Office, 1969.

Webb, J. P., & Willard, W. Six American Indian patterns of suicide. In N. L. Farberow (Ed.) *Suicide in different cultures*. Baltimore: University Park Press, 1975, 17-33.

Westermeyer, J. Disorganization. *American Journal of Psychiatry*, 1979, 128, 123-129.

Westermeyer, J., & Brantner, J. Violent death and alcohol use among the Chippewa of Minnesota. *Minnesota Medicine*, 1972, 55, 749-752

Chapter 9

Preventing Suicide in American Indians

Before examining the efforts which have been made to prevent suicide in American Indians, it would be useful to briefly review that major tactics for preventing suicide developed in nations around the world. In seeking to prevent suicide, we can divide our attack into three traditionally different goals: primary, secondary, and tertiary prevention. Let us look at each of these in turn.

Primary Prevention

Primary prevention involves the prevention of the *development* of suicidal tendencies in the individual. If we were able to prevent suicide in this way, people in the society would never become suicidal. This is, of course, the most difficult kind of prevention. It presupposes that we know the causes of suicide, which is doubtful, even after many years of scientific study. However, some suggestions can be made.

Psychiatric Disorder

Since a large proportion of suicides are psychiatrically disturbed, the primary prevention of psychiatric disturbance would go far toward preventing suicide. The same holds true for alcoholism and drug abuse. This, though, changes the problem to that of how can we prevent people from becoming psychiatrically disturbed or substance abusers.

For example, Barraclough (1972) examined one hundred cases of completed suicide and found that 64 had depressive illnesses. Of these, 44 had experienced previous depressive episodes, and 21 of these met strict criteria for a diagnosis of "recurrent affective illness." Barraclough noted that the suicide rate might have been reduced by 21 percent if these patients had been given lithium carbonate. Barraclough argued, therefore, for good diagnostic practices and the prescription of effective medication and, we might add, good psychotherapy as a way of preventing suicide.

Education

Rutz, et al. (1989) have shown that a program to educate physicians in the detection, evaluation and appropriate treatment of depression and suicide led to a reduction in the suicide rate on the island of Gotland (Sweden) as compared to the rest of Sweden. Eventually, without continued training, especially for physicians new to the island, the suicide rate rose again.

Educating the general public and, in particular, school children, about suicide has become popular in recent years, but the effectiveness of this tactic is in dispute (Shaffer, et al., 1988). Some suicide prevention workers are focusing on the research findings that suicidal tendencies are associated with low self-esteem and poor interpersonal skills. Thus, they are introducing programs into the schools whose goals is to improve the self-esteem of children and teach them better coping skills (Stivers, 1991). These school programs would seem to be more useful than those which seek merely to inform students and teachers about the clues to suicide and how to intervene with potentially suicidal individuals (Ryerson, 1991).

General Mental Health

Primary prevention might also focus on providing good general mental health services for communities and for groups with high rates of psychiatric disorder such as adolescent runaways. Many years ago Ratcliffe (1962) noted that changing a mental hospital from a locked-ward to an open-door system of patient management was accompanied by a drop in the number of suicides in the surrounding community, but a drop in the suicide rate does not always occur when community mental health centers are opened (Walk, 1967).

Survivors of Suicides

There are several groups at high risk for suicide, and early intervention with these groups might prevent suicide. For example, in the USA there has recently been a tremendous growth in groups for the relatives and loved-ones of those who have completed suicide. Work with these survivors of suicide promises to be a potentially powerful way of preventing suicide.

Childhood Trauma

It has been found that loss of a parent during the ages of six to fourteen is especially common in later suicides (Lester, 1989). If children who suffer such a loss were identified, perhaps at their schools, and given appropriate psychotherapy, their potential suicidal tendencies might be defused. Other childhood trauma have also been linked to later suicide, such as physical and sexual abuse (Lester, 1992). Children subjected to these assaults could aiso benefit from adequate psychotherapy, and a recent program to provide therapy for adolescents experiencing loss has been described by Hetzel, et al. (1991).

Predicting Suicides

In order to prevent suicide effectively in potential suicides, it is important that suicidologists improve their ability to predict suicide. We need to identify those with a high suicide risk at the societal level (by monitoring changing suicide trends in nations), the social level (by monitoring suicidal trends in groups such as the elderly, the divorced, and migrants), and at the individual level (by improving the psychological and psychiatric tests which predict individual suicidal risk).

In recent years, the excitement over the possibility of predicting suicidal behavior in future (Lester, 1970) has waned. Suicidologists have come to believe that prediction is not possible. The move has been toward *assessment* of suicidal individuals rather than *predicting* suicidal outcomes (Maris, et al., 1992). However, some researchers continue to work on suicide predictions scales both for completed suicides (Motto, et al., 1985) and repeat suicide attempts (Kreitman and Foster, 1991).

Epidemiological research may identify groups of the population with a high rate of suicide, but some of these groups have relatively few members. It may make more sense from a public policy point of view to focus suicide prevention efforts on larger groups, even though their suicide rates may be lower. Furthermore, epidemiological research should focus more on those variables which are amenable to change (such as social isolation) rather than those which are immutable but easily measured (such as sex and age).

Media Coverage of Suicide

It has been clearly demonstrated that media publicity about the suicides of famous suicides results in an increase for the next week in the suicide rate (Stack, 1990). Thus, care should be taken by the media in how they present news about suicides so that imitation is minimized. For example, publishing details of the method used and how it was obtained is dangerous. Glamorizing the suicide is likely to increase the suggestive impact of the suicide on others. Furthermore, researchers in the field have suggested that the media should always accompany suicide stories with information about suicide prevention resources in the community (Centers for Disease Control, 1988).

Comment

In general then, any program in a society which improves the general psychological health of its members may well prevent suicide and, we might note, other psychological and behavioral problems too. Hopefully, in the future, our understanding of suicide will have increased to the extent that we can make many more specific proposals for the primary prevention of suicide *per se*.

SECONDARY PREVENTION

Secondary prevention is early intervention with persons who are on the verge of suicide. Several strategies have been developed for this.

Suicide Prevention Centers

Suicide prevention centers have been set up in many countries in the world, and some nations have extensive networks of centers so that an individual always has a center near at hand. Suicide prevention centers typically have a 24-hour telephone crisis counseling service staffed by volunteer paraprofessionals. Some centers have, in addition, walk-in clinics and emergency outreach teams which can visit distressed individuals in the community.

This type of suicide prevention has been oriented around a crisis model of the suicidal process. People who are suicidal are conceptualized as being in a time-limited crisis state. Immediate crisis counseling will help the suicidal individual through the suicidal crisis, whereupon a normal life may resume.

Restricting Access to Lethal Methods for Suicide

Clarke and Lester (1989) have argued that restricting access to lethal methods for suicide might well reduce the suicide rate. They noted that this idea first gained prominence after the reduction in the English suicide rate by about a third in the 1960's and 1970's when domestic gas was detoxified by switching from coal gas (which contains carbon monoxide) to natural gas (which does not). They conducted a number of studies to show that the availability of firearms, toxic car exhaust and toxic domestic gas appears to be strongly related to the use of those methods for suicide, and that reducing the easy availability of these methods for suicide often reduced the overall suicide rate since not everyone switches methods for suicide when their preferred method becomes less easily available.

Clarke and Lester urged the detoxification of domestic gas, limits on the sales and ownership of firearms, restricting the size of medication prescriptions, placing the pills in plastic blisters which are hard to open, adding vomiting-inducing chemicals to medications so that an overdose will result in expulsion of the medication, prescription of suppositories rather than orally-taken tablets, prescribing the less toxic medications, cleaning up car emissions, changing the shape of the exhaust pipe to make it difficult to attach tubing, having an automatic engine turn-off mechanism if the car idles for more than a few minutes, fencing in bridges and high buildings from which people jump, and restricting the easy availability of herbicides and insecticides in developing countries.

It is worth noting that removing the means for suicide is a common strategy for hospitals in their efforts to prevent patients from committing suicide. Lester and Danto (1993) have recently described the use of this strategy in jails and prisons to reduce the incidence of inmate suicide.

Medical Emergency Services

Diggory (undated) has argued that we are preventing suicide with our emergency medical procedures. He estimated that in 1971, for example, the suicide rate in Pittsburgh was reduced from 15.2 to 12.5 (a reduction of 18 percent) simply by saving the lives of those who had attempted suicide. Thus, the improvement in emergency medical care in recent years has probably increased the extent to which those who might have died in the past from their suicidal actions now survive.

TERTIARY PREVENTION

Tertiary prevention is the prevention of the recurrence of suicide in those who have already been suicidal. Strictly speaking there is no tertiary prevention for completed suicide. A completed suicide is dead. We can help only those who are not yet dead by their own hand. However, if we bear in mind that some people who seriously intend to kill themselves are thwarted by the intervention of others and by emergency medical treatment, then we can talk about preventing the recurrence of suicidal behavior in these individuals.

On the other hand, such individuals constitute the group which we label attempted suicides or parasuicides. Tertiary prevention then might involve distinguishing carefully between those who are making suicidal gestures and those who would have died but for intervention. This latter group, once identified, could be made the target population for intensive tertiary prevention efforts, which in this case would resemble secondary prevention methods.

Available research shows that psychiatric treatment may be beneficial here. Several reviews of which medications appear to be best for suicidal clients have appeared (for example, Schifano and De Leo, 1991). Recently, counseling strategies specifically oriented toward suicidal clients have been proposed, for example, Clum and Lerner (1990). Further research on tertiary prevention should focus on which medications and counseling techniques are most effective for treating seriously suicidal people who have made lethal attempts to kill themselves.

One other suggestion for tertiary prevention is to investigate the environments into which these serious attempters are released. Does their environment contain suicidogenic stresses, hostile significant others who increase the likelihood of self-destructive desires, or lethal means for suicide? One suicide prevention center in the USA used to search the homes of attempted suicides, removing all guns, large knives, poisons and lethal drugs. They were able to do this, of course, only for attempted suicides who contacted them, and they did it with the tolerance of the local police force. It is not a technique that is likely to be available to most preventers of suicide, but it does illustrate a technique for tertiary prevention.

Preventing Suicide in American Indians

Webb and Willard (1975) argued that we cannot assume that suicide prevention techniques devised for the general American culture will be useful for American Indians. For example, many American Indian groups feel most uncomfortable talking about feelings to non-group members, and so a telephone crisis intervention service may not be utilized by American Indians, even if telephones were available in the areas in which they live. Language may also be a barrier for American Indians, who might prefer talking in their native tongue rather than English.

McIntosh and Santos (1984) noted that ethnic minorities in general may not utilize mental health services as much as whites. The reasons for this include language problems, the stigma attached in the culture to needing such services, limited access, and low awareness of the services which are available. Added to this, minorities may distrust white mental health professionals and, indeed, may have been treated insensitively, and even humiliated, in their previous contacts with whites.

Earls, et al. (1990) reviewed intervention strategies that had been tried in American Indian communities. Nearly three-quarters had focused on primary prevention in the area of general mental health, including education, training, recreation and sociocultural programs, such as increasing the proportion of American Indian house-parents for boarding school students and training dormitory aides in techniques for encouraging positive behaviors in the students.

Some intervention efforts focused on counseling and providing facilities for American Indians at high risk for suicide, such a medical holding facility for those arrested for drunk and disorderly behavior as an alternative to jail. Only a minority of the programs worked with suicidal individuals directly, such as establishing suicide registers, crisis hotlines and psychotherapy with attempted suicides.

Earls felt that American Indian communities prefer the primary intervention programs because they are non-stigmatizing and because they emphasize collective activity by the community. However, their benefits are long-term and are not cost-effective for suicide prevention. Health care organizations prefer the more direct programs which are more easily set up, relate more directly to patient needs, and can be credited to an agency.

However, a word of caution is warranted here about being overly critical of conventional psychiatric and public health approaches to suicidal behavior and other psychiatric problems in American Indians. As Thompson, et al. (1993) have noted, conventional approaches for treatment and prevention have not been established in a satisfactory manner on American Indian reservations and have not adequately evaluated as yet. It may premature to urge their abandonment. Neligh (1988) also argued forcefully that the traditional techniques have not been provided for these communities and that, before we discard them, they ought to be tried, particularly since the Indian Health Service exists and could provide a good base for such services.

Neligh noted that suicide prevention efforts should distinguish between epidemics of suicide and endemic patterns of suicide. Epidemics lead to attention being focused on a community, but epidemics are time-limited by definition, and so prevention efforts will be hard to evaluate since the suicides will decrease in frequency after a time no matter what is done. In contrast, endemic patterns, the steady ongoing suicide rate in a community, can be addressed by suicide prevention programs and the success of these programs evaluated. May (1967), for example, noted that the Navajo pattern of suicide was endemic whereas the Apache pattern was similar to an epidemic pattern.

American Indian Involvement

May and Dizmang (1974) have argued against the imposition of Western values by agencies, including the Federal Government. American Indians need to be given an active role in deciding what to do and in influencing their fate. American Indians must be involved in policy making concerning education, community action, and mental health programs. Self-determination must guide the restructuring of their societies.

A similar point has been made by Davenport and Davenport (1987). They urged interveners to strengthen community solidarity and social cohesion in Indian tribes, to support their values and practices, and to develop a social structure which is valued by the Indians. Thus, American Indians must be consulted about these changes and, indeed, take a leading role in planning and implementing them. Davenport and Davenport warned against using American Indians who have assimilated into the larger culture who may not understand the less assimilated Indian, and they noted that tribal rivalries must be considered. People from one tribe may not be able to work effectively with people from another tribe. American Indians must determine the nature and form of their society, and outsiders must work only *with* the American Indians, not *for* them. If we must, for the time being, provide crisis intervention and counseling and psychotherapy for those in need, outsiders must work to train American Indians to work in these services, to determine the direction of the programs and eventually to take over the administration of the programs.

Dizmang (1966) stressed the importance of discovering who are the gatekeepers in each community. In the Cheyenne community he visited in Montana after three boys had unsuccessfully tried to shoot themselves, he found that the VISTA volunteers, the clergy and the community health workers were the gatekeepers. Dizmang suggested training these gatekeepers in crisis intervention and providing them with adequate back-up when consultation was necessary. Mindell and Stuart (1969) also suggested getting community gatekeepers involved, people such as community leaders and medicine men, even in the case conferences concerning clients in crisis. They suggested setting up Community Service Centers where all of the resources could be located (possibly near post offices) so that local community groups would have a center around which to grow.

Charles (1991) urged the pairing of young people in crisis with community elders during times of crisis so that traditional values will be enhanced at the same time that coping skills are learned. In this way, there is less danger of imposing non-American Indian intervention styles on people who discourage introspection and consider a preoccupation with the self to be a threat to tribal and family values.

Rural Community Health Programs

Mindell and Stuart (1969) cautioned against trying to apply urban techniques for suicide prevention to Indian reservations which are predominantly rural. On reservations, there is a lack of easy transportation such as mass transit, communication (such as the telephone) and agency resources for the residents, although there is a large support network comprising mainly of relatives. Clients often fail to show regularly for appointments and, when they do show, it is often difficult to find appropriate resources for them, such as employment, housing, training or shelter situations (halfway houses, etc.).

Kinzie, et al. (1972) also noted that the rural nature of many American Indian communities may make traditional strategies for delivering mental health care inappropriate. Furthermore, American Indians have several agencies with authority, and great care must be taken in establishing mental health services to involve them all.

To illustrate this process, Kinzie described a program which he established to provided psychiatric consultation and care to a rural village in the Pacific Northwest with a population of about 500 people, 250 of whom were children. The village was on the coast, and the tribe had hunted whales for a living. They had been aggressive and warlike and had ceremonial feasts in which they gave possessions away (potlatch). The arrival of the government in the 1800's resulted in the prohibition of tribal customs, forced education in English-language boarding schools, and led to a shift from whaling to fishing and agriculture. The village remained isolated until a road was built in the 1930's. (The village is 50 miles from the nearest town and 150 miles from psychiatric resources.) Since the Indian Reorganization Act, the Tribal Council has become powerful and, though the tribe is still poor and somewhat culturally disorganized, the Indian tradition has remained viable.

About 35% of the community was diagnosed with alcoholism, and a further 22% had psychosomatic illnesses, primarily peptic ulcer. Alcoholism, however, was not viewed as a psychiatric problem by the community, and so medical help was not sought.

The team first spent time learning about the sociocultural nature of the community, and then sought the approval of the relevant governing bodies. They discussed their proposal with the Indian Health Service (of the United States Public Health Service) and the Bureau of Indian Affairs. After these two agencies approved the program, the team met with the Tribal Council. This preliminary work of orientation and negotiation took six months.

The community had a medical clinic, staffed by a physician and a local Indian nurse. There were also two Indian Community Health Representatives who lived locally, attached to the clinic. This clinic was viewed positively by the community, but the local social workers and counselors were not. The team worked through the medical clinic and trained the health representatives in crisis intervention so that they became psychiatric aides. Eventually, the two health representatives moved to the tribal headquarters.

The team made contact with the other agencies in the community -- the school administrators and counselor, the welfare worker, the Head Start teachers and parents, the local Indian police, and the Indian Community Action program. The school and welfare workers were more willing to cooperate than were the other agencies.

In the first six months, the team provided mostly consultation, but they also provided diagnostic services and occasionally brief crisis intervention. These latter cases were then transferred to the health representatives or the medical clinic for continued care. The patients were reasonably amenable to psychodynamically-oriented brief therapy. About half of the first few patients were referred by the medical clinic and health representatives, while others came by themselves having heard about the services. The patients were primarily young adult women, but there were four adolescent males. The adult women were primarily depressed and anxious; the teenage boys showed delinquent or disruptive school behavior. There were eleven suicide attempts during the first six-month period involving seven people (three adult females, three adult males and one adolescent male). The females and the adolescent were diagnosed as having reactive depressions, the adult males as alcoholics. The three adult males rejected all psychiatric referrals.

In the first six months, the team had 152 contacts, 52 directly with patients. The team functioned well with case consultation and direct patient contact but were less successful in promoting agency interaction. The Tribal Council and government agencies were pleased with the program and requested a continued consultation program.

Primary Prevention for American Indian Suicide

A great deal of effort has focused on preventing suicide in American Indians, and many of these efforts have involved primary prevention. For example, the Alaska state legislature supported 54 projects in 1989 for community-initiated suicide prevention programs (Young, et al., 1992). One third involved improving communication between elders and youth; others provided recreational alternatives, strengthening support and self-help networks, and developing cultural projects.

Thompson (1989) made the following general suggestions for the primary prevention of American Indian suicide: (1) improving socioeconomic conditions for American Indians, (2) recognizing and treating the underlying psychiatric disorders, (3) coordinating the health and mental health services and working with other agencies in the community such as schools, police and tribal councils, and (4) addressing the cultural conflicts especially in American Indian youth.

A good example of primary prevention is provided by Ward (1984). He described the program set up on an Objibway Canadian Indian reservation.

The reservation was an island, largely rural and quite isolated, and suicide was especially common in one small community of some 200 people. There had been a good deal of acculturation, for the Jesuits had been present since the 1600's.

The child-rearing style was to let children learn by modeling themselves on the parents rather than shaping the child's behavior. Thus, the children were often regarded as backward and uncooperative in school. The practice of sending the children away to boarding schools in the past had created a generation of parents who today had little understanding of their culture and who were conflicted in their child-rearing tactics. Alcohol abuse was common, and a pattern of heavy drinking was typically established by the age of fourteen.

Ward described several features of an ideal suicide prevention program. It must be multidimensional, and it must focus on general problems in the community. Canadian Indians should be involved in running the program as much as possible so that the administrators and counselors can understand the values and attitudes of the clients. The program must deal with the negative identity which has developed about being a Canadian Indian and the loss of tradition and history. Since alcohol abuse is a major problem, the program must deal with this, treating it as a social problem rather than an individual problem. Finally, the program must target key groups in the community -- the children, mothers, wives, and men.

The program developed with the establishment of the Rainbow Lodge Alcohol Recovery Program. The director and staff were Canadian Indians, and the residential program was modeled on Alcoholics Anonymous, but changed to fit with the needs of Canadian Indians. The lodge eventually set up youth programs, including alcohol education lessons for school children, classes to educate adults on parenting skills, and cultural enrichment programs which encouraged the continuation of traditional activities and festivals. There was also a mental health clinic and a crisis intervention service for those in need. Although there was no formal evaluation of the program, Ward noted that both fatal and nonfatal suicidal declined after the lodge was established.

Berlin (1985, 1987) has described residential alcohol treatment centers which bring families to the center for treatment and plan work and recreational programs for the suicidal adolescents. Programs for alcohol abusers and depressed or hostile individual should be sanctioned by the tribal leaders, healers and elders of the tribe and should use American Indian staff. Berlin noted the usefulness of programs such as referring first-time offenders, especially drug or alcohol abusing youths, to family therapy rather than to the criminal justice system. High-risk female adolescents can be offered child care jobs, encouraged to remain in school, and participate in seminars on child-rearing and development led by tribal mental health professionals. Pregnant women, and pregnant high school girls in particular, can be given classes on parenting and work in day-care centers, and the fathers-to-be can be encouraged to attend. Classes can also extend beyond the birth of the child, so that mothers learn how to cope with problems such as crying and fussy babies. Berlin urged that schools and tribal gatekeepers make greater efforts to identify adolescents at high risk of suicide because of their family background, traumatic experiences, and behavior so that early intervention can be attempted. In high schools, it is not simply the depressed students who may need help. For example, in one school some successful girls who became cheerleaders and debate captains were harassed by others because they "stood out." Several made suicide attempts. Tribal leaders were brought in to support the need to be good learners and leaders, and support groups were set up for these girls. Berlin also noted a program which took high-risk female adolescents and trained them to become counselors for difficult children. They used their experiences with the children to explore and come to terms with their own personal childhood trauma. In all of these activities, Berlin emphasized that the approval of tribal leaders was critical and that issues of confidentiality must be confronted more actively than with white clients.

Charles (1991) has also urged primary prevention. He has advocated the strengthening of family bonds and the re-establishment of traditional extended-family networks. Education in parenting through prenatal classes, parenting class, and parenting support groups might lead to a healthier home environment for children. Getting the community to accept these programs involves them understanding the extent of suicide and other self-destructive behaviors in their communities, and so requires education through community forums. Charles also recommended the development of social and recreational activities to improve the quality of life in the communities.

DeBruyn, et al. (1994) focused on primary prevention in their adolescent suicide prevention project with the Apache (Jicarilla) where their initial suicide prevention effort grew into a community-based integrated set of programs to combat suicide, domestic violence and child abuse and to promote parenting skills and developing wellness.

Restoration of Traditional Culture

Many of those discussing the prevention of suicide among American Indians have urged the restoration of the traditional culture. For example, Long (1986) urged the reinstatement of cultural traditions on the reservations, since these rituals and ceremonies forge a sense of community and reduce the feelings of powerlessness. In the reservation where she worked, religious groups planned traditional forms of recreation for the youths and restored the traditional rites of passage for them.

French and Hornbuckle (1979) described a "cultural therapy" program, begun on the Qualla Reservation with the Cherokee as a response to high rates of alcohol abuse and suicide, which involved informally structured cultural sessions focusing on arts and crafts. The goals were to increases clients' integration back in to the community by reinforcing their sense of belonging, to strengthen the clients' awareness of their cultural heritage, and to provide acceptable avenues for tension management and release. The construction of Cherokee cultural objects increase the clients' self-esteem without the stigma that often accompanies participation in mental health treatment programs. French and Hornbuckle saw the approach as similar to network therapy (Speck and Rueveni, 1969), but with an emphasis on the collective system common to American Indians rather than focusing on personal guilt as in western systems.

Diversion

It has been documented that many American Indian youths commit suicide in jail after committing minor offenses, especially when drunk. Ogden, et al. (1970) briefly described a program on Idaho's Fort Hall Indian Reservation in which intoxicated American Indians were placed in a special detoxification unit run by the Indian Health Service rather than in a jail run by the criminal justice system. Medical treatment and counseling by volunteers from the American Indian community reduced the risk of suicide. The youths were then referred for psychotherapy if needed, with a social worker and consultant psychiatrist provided by the Indian Health Service.

An alternative to diversion from jail has been to ask tribal elders to stay with the youth in the jail cell overnight and to provide counseling for them, making the youths feel like valuable members of the tribe (Shore, et al., 1972). Female tribal elders have been recruited to stay with the families in which an adolescent girl has attempted suicide to act as a listener and advocate (Red Horse, 1982).

Psychiatric Disorder

Neligh (1988) noted that depression is common among American Indians and panic attacks are found also, both syndromes associated with a high risk for suicide. If these, and other, major psychiatric illnesses were treated, then suicide rates may well fall in American Indian communities. The mental health professionals servicing American Indians and community leaders and gatekeepers would need to be alerted and trained to recognize the symptoms of psychiatric disorder, and adequate and acceptable treatment resources need to be established. Opportunities for hospitalization and the development of social support networks need to be established also, including self-help groups.

The prevention of drug and alcohol abuse would go far in preventing suicide, as would the establishment of bereavement groups and other resources for the bereaved. Despite clinic policies, Neligh found that emergency rooms often treat attempted suicides for the medical damage and release them without any referral for psychological counseling or psychiatric treatment.

Finally, Neligh noted that identifying high risk groups and targeting them for intervention might also prevent suicide -- such as young men between 16 and 20 years of age who are depressed and drink excessively. This requires adequate monitoring of psychiatric symptoms among the population by well-trained epidemiologists.

SECONDARY PREVENTION FOR AMERICAN INDIAN SUICIDE

Blanchard, et al. (1976) suggested the following guidelines for suicide prevention on reservations: (1) that each village maintain a 24-hour crisis center, (2) that motivated American Indians run the centers trained for both telephone and face-to-face crisis counseling, (3) that the centers maintain a list of suicidal individuals in their village and that special community workers be assigned to work with these individuals, (4) that people be trained in emergency medical care and provided with an ambulance so that potential suicides can be saved, (5) that the tribal police be trained in suicide prevention, (6) that the Public Health Service provide 24-hour medical, psychiatric and psychological consulting and services, (7) that the Bureau of Indian Affairs become involved with these efforts, (8) that emergency telephones be placed at strategic places throughout the reservations, (9) that the schools get involved with these efforts, and (10) that tribal leaders be encouraged to get involved in these efforts.

Telephone Crisis Counseling

For the one million American Indians served by the Indian Health Service, about 37% of the households were without a telephone in 1980 (as compared to only 8% for the United States as a whole), but in some areas the percentage was even higher -- 75% of the Navajo households were without a telephone (Rhoades, et al., 1987).

This does not mean that it is impossible to provide a telephone service. For example, a telephone has placed on some bridges in both America and England which potential suicidal jumpers can use to obtain immediate contact with a crisis counselor. One lifts up the telephone, and the crisis center is automatically contacted. Telephones with this restricted access could be placed at strategic locations around a reservation.

In Australia, a toll-free number has been allocated to suicide prevention centers, so that anyone may call free of charge and the system automatically connects the caller to the nearest suicide prevention center. If the counselors at that center are busy, the call is transferred to the closest center with an available counselor. Even though there are fewer households with telephones on reservations than in American households in general, at least some American Indians would have easy access to a telephone crisis counselor if such a system were established.

Charles (1991) suggested that crisis centers should have the facilities for short-term residential crisis treatment to be used when necessary, and such facilities make have some utility, especially if staffed by American Indians.

Prince (1988) noted that four crisis intervention and suicide prevention programs had been set up by the time he was writing on Canadian reservation, two in British Columbia, one in Saskatchewan and one in Toronto. These centers appear to have provided counseling, health promotion information, and information on how to improve Indian-non-Indian relations.

School Programs

Berlin (1990) set up a program in four high schools for American Indian girls at high risk for suicide: they had a sharp decline in their academic performance, were increasingly truant, had chaotic families with at least one alcoholic parent and had been picked up for disorderly behavior when drunk. The girls were paid an hourly minimum wage for attending two group meetings of one-and-a-half hours each week where the curriculum covered parenting skills, the psychology of sexuality, decision making, drug and alcohol education and traditional views on unwed pregnancy, alcohol and suicide presented by medicine men.

The program lasted two years, and there were drop-outs and replacements. Ten percent of the girls became pregnant compared with 30% in the larger community, grades improved slightly, there was no involvement with the law, and 90% of those drinking had cut down to no more than once a month. Only three of the girls attempted suicide.

LaFromboise and Howard-Pitney (1994) devised a suicide prevention program for schools on the Zuni reservation. The program taught life skills (including communication skills, problem-solving, and stress and anger regulation) in addition to the more standard suicide prevention content (identification of common warning signs associated with the suicide, active listening, and referral to community resources). The program was also tailored to the Zuni by inclusion of culturally-relevant material and team-teaching with Zuni community resource people. A pilot study of the program showed that students who took the program had lowered scores on a measure of suicide potential as compared to a control group who did not take them program.

Identifying High Risk Groups

May (1987) described the steps taken by an Intermountain group of American Indians with whom he consulted. The tribe set up a facility for counseling and supporting youths considered at risk for suicide, where they could stay. Officials on the reservation (including police and health staff) were encouraged to refer youths to the facility.

However, the Tribal Council then broadened its approach and moved to primary prevention. It sought grants and funding for further programs, and the mental health resources of the community were increased. Housing funds were obtained, and recreational facilities built, including a new gym, baseball fields, and festival and rodeo grounds. Arrangements were made to educate more of the children on the reservation. New tribal businesses were created, including a supermarket, a craft store and a tribal restaurant and gas station, attracting many tourists from the local interstate highway.

Tribal advocacy for its interests has improved, and the tribal has worked to protect its land base and hunting rights. Its bison herd has increased from a less than a dozen animals to over 400. Tribal services have been improved and increasingly staffed by members of the tribe.

Comment

Levy and Kunitz (1987), noting the stigma attached among the Hopi to being labeled as suicidal (or alcohol abuser), recommended that suicide prevention programs not be so labeled and not be part of the Indian Health Service of tribal health delivery system. Levy and Kunitz recommended focusing the program on education and activities, minimizing the involvement of professionals and maximizing the role of community volunteers. As an example of a good program using these criteria, they mentioned wilderness adventure programs for distressed youth.

The Role of Outside Professionals in Preventing American Indian Suicide

Several commentators have discussed the role of outside professionals in programs designed to prevent American Indian suicide. For example, Long (1986) has discussed the role of the nurse in suicide prevention in American Indian communities. As health professionals, nurses can serve leadership roles, especially in the supervision of American Indian health aides (though it would seem to the present author to be more important to train American Indians to become nurses themselves). Long notes that American Indian health aides understand the community values and customs better and are more accepted by the community members.

Jordan (1988) has warned professionals to be sensitive to the possibility that standardized psychological tests and psychiatric interview and diagnostic systems may need modification for American Indians. For example, the Minnesota Multiphasic Personality Inventory (MMPI) may need to be interpreted differently for American Indians (Pollack and Shore, 1980), and the criteria for depression may have to be changed, especially with regard to the length of time symptoms persist.

Psychotherapy places a high value on vocabulary, self-disclosure, introspection and a desire for and active involvement in change of the self. These traits are not common among American Indians who, therefore, appear to be passive and "resistant" to western counselors. The theory of mental illness for the American Indian may differ from western views; for example, some American Indian tribes believe that mental illness can arise from spirit possession and from transgressions. Clients who believe this may benefit more from a healer from their culture than from a western-oriented counselor.

Jordan felt that one system of therapy in particular may be suitable for American Indians, namely existential therapy. Existential therapy focuses on death, isolation, meaningless and freedom, issues which are easy for American Indians to understand. Death crises occur more often for American Indians and at an earlier age and, furthermore, the deaths of their ancestors (which came close to genocide) remains a powerful tribal memory. American Indians are aware of their isolation from the mainstream culture. They are both isolated geographically and suffer from racism. Meaningless is a major issue as the American Indian confronts the issue of acculturation (adopting western values) versus assimilation (adapting to western culture while preserving one's own culture). How can the American Indian find meaning as an American Indian in this society? The issue of freedom comes up in the perception of control. Does the Anglo culture have control over the American Indian's fate, or can the American Indian wrest some control back? Suicide by the American Indian, for example, may be viewed as seeking freedom in death.

Jordan also thought that cognitive therapy, and also family and group therapy, may be useful for American Indians, but their techniques may require modification, especially family and group therapy, for American Indians may not be comfortable discussing personal issues in a "public" setting.

Finally, Jordan urged the integration of western systems of counseling traditional American Indian healing ceremonies, such as medicine ceremonies, sweat lodges and talking circles. A "team" approach, combining western-oriented and American Indian healers together, may help clients more than either acting alone.

The Indian Health Service established a Special Initiatives Team in 1987 to provide consultation to American Indian communities requesting advice and consultation about any mental health problem (DeBruyn, et al., 1988). The team visits the community, assesses the needs of the community, and makes recommendations as to the steps that the community should take. In one instance, a community requesting advice on dealing with suicide, child abuse and violence was encouraged to set up a social services program and the director was assisted in making visits to other facilities in order to obtain ideas on how to organize the program.

Mindell and Stuart (1968) gave examples of their consultation to help develop new programs, to assist the coordination of resources, and to make the existing services more responsive to local needs. As we have already noted in this chapter, the rural nature of many American Indian reservations makes transportation, communication and delivery of services difficult. The communities also lack the resources available to urban communities in America, such as employment services and halfway houses. Thus, staff often feel great frustration working in these settings and may need help to deal with their feelings.

EXAMPLES OF SUCCESSFUL SUICIDE PREVENTION PROGRAMS

Shore, et al. (1972) have described the establishment of a suicide prevention program for a group of Plains Indians from a variety of bands, numbering about 3,000, on a reservation of about half a million acres. From 1961 to 1986, the suicide rate was 98 per 100,000 per year. This high rate of suicide (with an even higher rate of suicide attempts -- in one particular month there were thirty suicide attempts) prompted the tribal council to ask the Indian Health Service and the Bureau of Indian Affairs for assistance. Consultants from the National Institute of Mental Health and from the Los Angeles suicide prevention center recommended the establishment of a facility where people in crisis could stay for up to 24 hours. Community participation was stressed, Indian volunteers recruited, and the Indian Health Service building provided the holding facility. The tribal health committee participated in the plans and the recruitment of staff. Professional coverage was provided by the social workers from the Indian Health Service and the Bureau of Indian Affairs.

In the first thirteen months of operation, there were 36 admissions involving 30 people. Twenty four of the admissions were under the age of 25, and thirty involved suicidal attempts or threats. Seventeen of the 30 patients were men, 44% had been drinking, and 31% sniffing glue or solvents. Twenty-nine percent came from the jail, while some were brought directly by the police.

A social worker and physician evaluated the patient immediately after admission. The volunteer counselors and family members then spent time with the patient, often conversing in the Indian language. Intoxicated, often combative, patients soon quieted down and, with the consultation of the social workers, a plan devised. Most of the patients were released to their families, and follow-up appointments arranged. A few returned to jail, a few to inpatient settings. Unfortunately, Shore did not give details of the treatment plans.

Kahn and Delk (1973) described the development of a psychological services clinic on the Papago Indian Reservation. The initial plan was for a community mental health service which would consult with other persons and agencies, employ Papago Indians wherever possible, consult with Papago medicine men, and develop groups for alcoholism and marital problems. The planning team made sure that the tribal council and the Indian Health Service approved the plans.

Initially, there were few Papago Indians on the staff, not enough availability of the student volunteers for the program, and difficulty in meeting the needs of a widespread population. A traveling clinic was set up which did not function well but served to give everyone involved some experience with the community and its problems. By the end of the first year, the first Papago staff member was in training, and he worked with two white psychological consultants and two white clinical psychology graduate students.

Eventually, there were five Papago staff members, as well as a social worker and secretary.

The service consulted with the various schools in the community, set up groups for delinquent youth and those involved with drugs, consulted with the medical hospital, developed counseling services for the teen center, and consulted with many of the reservation agencies. In a follow-up report seventeen years after the establishment of the service, Kahn, et al. (1988) reported that the service was now run by Papago staff who used the consultants only as a last resort. The service had about two hundred clients a year, and it had decided to deal with clients who could not come to the center by using two-way radios since telephones were scarce in some parts of the reservation.

The major problem faced by the service was having to deal with off-reservation agencies when they needed their help with clients, such as those who needed psychiatric hospitalization. The public agencies did not trust Papago staff evaluations and insisted on doing their own evaluations. The white staff at these agencies had difficulty interacting with Papago Indians, often not understanding their behavioral style or language. Occasionally they would refuse to work with the patients, and the Papago staff then had to take the patients back to reservation after a time-consuming and humiliating experience at the hands of the agency. Kahn noted that the private agencies were much more helpful, though of course more expensive.

Kahn gave up trying to change the attitudes of the public agencies in the state and concluded that the reservation needed its own residential crisis center and halfway house facility so that it could handle patients with more serious problems on the reservation.

LEARNING FROM A STUDY OF FAILURES

Berman (1980) detailed the failures of the Duck Valley Reservation in Nevada to respond to its suicide problem, and we can learn much from this account. The reservation, 293,000 acres and quite isolated, was home to about one thousand Shoshoni and Paiute who were combined into one "tribe" by the government in 1938. The tribal government suffered from factionalism because of tribal rivalry; the Bureau of Indian Affairs had a policy of non-interference unless asked for help; the Indian Health Services Hospital was staffed by visiting physicians with only a two-year tenure who underutilized American Indian staff and who were distrusted by the American Indians. The hospital refused to treat alcohol abusers (the reservation lacks a detoxification unit), a policy that Berman called "unconscionable."

Berman noted that the American Indian culture also contributed to the problem. The strong family structure helped fuel the lack of group cohesion, even in the tribal elections where the results have implications for family power. Self-advancement takes second place to working for the family. Making a profit, for example, in business diminishes the person unless the success is shared with family members. Educational achievement is also antithetical to the family. If successful students return to the reservation, there is no use for their skills. If they leave the reservation, they are viewed as having "copped out." The small population and extended families also hinder protecting confidentiality in any mental health service since gossip about clients will soon spread around the reservation.

Yet the reservation had a mental health problem. Berman calculated the suicide rate from 1949-1978 as 117 per 100,000 per year (and about 300 for those aged 15-24). The suicides had a median age of 23, were predominantly male, were alcohol related, and used firearms. From 1972-1978, there were about ten officially-noted suicide attempts per year (compared to 1.2 completed suicides per year), 59% by women.

After four suicides in 1969, the tribal council established a mental health committee. A grant was obtained to study the problem, and recommendations made. A recreational therapist was hired, and recreational services established. This therapist left in the mid 1970's and was not replaced. Proposals for a cultural enrichment center, mental health programs in crisis intervention, an on-reservation nursing home, and a study of the educational system were not implemented. In 1975, all children in grades seven through twelve were screened with a psychological inventory and high-risk children identified, but no program was instituted for them.

Berman made a number of recommendations for the Duck Valley Reservation, though the usefulness of these was questionable given the inability of the leaders to implement any previous recommendations! Berman recommended:

(1) That the tribal council and Bureau of Indian Affairs plan economic development and incentives for the reservation, (2) that the tribal council hire a consultant to follow-through with the agencies who might fund programs, (3) that a consultant be hired to help the tribal leaders work with the community factions, and (4) that the Bureau of Indian Affairs take an active position in teaching grantsmanship and management skills to the tribal leaders.

With respect to suicide prevention, Berman urged (1) that the Indian Health Service set up and implement crisis intervention and management services, (2) that a holding facility be set up for emergency interventions, (3) that an alcohol detoxification center be established so that alcohol abusers were no longer placed in jail, (4) that staff physicians and others be educated regarding alcohol abuse and suicide prevention and, in addition, trained about the problems of confidentiality with this population, (5) that a data bank regarding suicidal behavior and other critical psychiatric problems be established that involved all of the community agencies (school, criminal justice and health), (6) that a team be established for conducting psychological autopsies into suicidal and other deaths and for providing help to the survivors, (7) that funding be sought for the establishment of an indigenous mental health team, (8) that a program be established for identifying and helping high-risk children, (9) that follow-up services be provided for all suicide attempters and threateners, (10) that American Indians be recruited to train indigenous staff, (11) that an American Indian Studies program and Archival Center be established to develop programs on American Indian culture which would involve members of the community and develop a sense of pride in the members of the community, and (12) that recreational opportunities be established to provide meaningful alternatives to drinking.

Consultation with American Indian groups is not always easy. Tyler, et al. (1982) discussed some of the problems they encountered as consultants to a reservation in North Dakota. The consultant from the university visited the reservation twice a month accompanied by two or three graduate students who worked on the project for a year, a service paid for by the tribal government. Tyler's goal was to consult rather than provide direct client service and to focus on primary and secondary prevention. A Youth Council was formed which involved members from various reservation agencies and served to promote coordination. Community education workshops were given, and consultation provided to reservation staff.

One problem that Tyler encountered was that the values on the reservation were not homogeneous. While the oldest and youngest members believed that traditional ways were the best, the adults had invested themselves in the contemporary mainstream culture. Furthermore, the traditional expectations did not always fit the residents, and traditional customs and values were in flux. For example, the residents were not clear any more whether maintaining or avoiding eye contact enhanced interpersonal communication. Nonetheless, Tyler observed the general values of individual freedom, preference for behavioral over verbal expression, respect for age, present orientation, preference for cooperation over competition, and a lack of stress on scheduling.

Although Tyler agreed that native counselors and paraprofessionals were of great value, they also posed problems. The natives were members of the community and so knew their neighbors and were well-known., Thus, problems of objectivity and confidentiality arose, especially for the clients who did not trust the counselors. The paraprofessionals were often poorly educated and so could not be used to provide more expert services. They sometimes quit their positions prematurely because of political and economic factors in the community and the pressure from the community to let others have the positions after a while.

The native clients seemed to prefer brief interventions and often dropped out if assigned to extended treatment. This was partly due to the difficulties of transportation on the reservation, to the distrust of white mental health approaches, and to a general dislike for scheduling. Three or four sessions while in crisis was the best for clients. Tyler noted that there were no medicine men on the reservation, and so cooperation with them was not an option.

The community came to accept the program after five years or so when they realized that the consultants would not be like those in the past who had left after a few months. The community also came to accept the transient graduate students, though the feeling was that the services provided were second-rate compared to those offered whites.

Levy (1988) also discussed the problems which arise in preventing suicide among American Indians. Research on suicidal behavior among the Shoshoni-Bannock indicated that none of the completed suicides had made prior suicide attempts and that the suicides were found in only eight of the families on the reservation. The majority of the suicides, going back into the 19th Century, came from only four families. These families had been labeled as deviants and had become scapegoats for the community. Just as one particular family member may be the symptom bearer for a whole family, so in this community these families seemed to bear the symptoms for the community. Thus, an effective suicide prevention program would not be one which focused on high risk youth, such as those who had attempted suicide, but rather one which focused on getting to know these few families intimately and working with them to change their status. However, to focus efforts on these families might serve to reinforce their "labeled" status as deviants.

Among the Hopi, Levy found that suicide was not a result of acculturation stress or anomie, but rather concentrated in the children of families who had made deviant marriages, such as when high status female American Indians took low status male mates who later laid claim to prestigious ceremonial positions. However, to overtly deal with this problem would be to alienate the Hopi. Levy suggested that a successful suicide prevention program needed to appeal to both deviant and non-deviant people in the community, and to avoid identifying with the existing treatment programs or with any theory of the cause of Hopi problems.

Discussion

It can be seen from this chapter that there has been a great deal of effort directed toward preventing American Indian suicide, and it appears that the majority of the efforts have been made in the area of primary prevention, a contrast to the suicidology movement in America as a whole where secondary prevention has been stressed. This emphasis on primary prevention for American Indians is useful because, not only may it eventually have an impact on suicidal behavior, but it may also have an impact on other maladaptive behaviors such as drug and alcohol abuse and delinquency.

The reports on prevention efforts, however, do lack an adequate evaluation component. Even when the program described appears to have worked well, there are rarely any objective data presented to show that the program helped the individuals on the reservation -- whether alcohol abuse or domestic violence declined as a result of the efforts, for example. It is, therefore, impossible at the present time to distinguish those approaches and programs that have been effective from those which have not. To take just one example, the establishment of telephone suicide prevention and crisis intervention services, we cannot say whether such a service is feasible, whether public telephones or a toll-free number would facilitate their use, to what extent they would be used, etc. Commentators have argued for and against the establishment of these services without such data to guide their speculations. One would have expected that, by now, several such services would have been set up, using different strategies, and that data had been collected and published on the volume of calls, the satisfaction of clients, and the organizational and administrative problems. This would have enabled suicide prevention centers to improve their services and permitted communities planning such centers to learn from the experiences of others.

References

Barraclough, B. M. Suicide prevention, recurrent affective disorder and lithium. *British Journal of Psychiatry*, 1972, 121, 391-392.

Berlin, I. N. Prevention of adolescent suicide among some Native American tribes. *Adolescent Psychiatry*, 1985, 12, 77-93.

Berlin, I. N. Suicide among American Indian adolescents. *Suicide & Life-Threatening Behavior*, 1987, 17, 218-232.

Berlin, I. N. Reduced suicide attempts in high risk Indian female adolescents. In D. Lester (Ed.) *Suicide '90*. Denver, CO: American Association of Suicidology, 1990, 286-287.

Berman, A. L. Indian suicide. *Nevada Public Affairs Review*, 1980, #1, 24-31.

Blanchard, J. D., Blanchard, E. L., & Roll, S. A psychological autopsy of an Indian adolescent suicide with implications for community services. *Suicide & Life-Threatening Behavior*, 1976, 6, 3-10.

Centers for Disease Control. CDC recommendations for a community plan for the prevention and containment of suicide clusters. *Morbidity & Mortality Weekly Report*, 1988, 37, (supplement # 5-6), 1-12.

Charles, G. Suicide intervention and prevention among Northern Native youth. *Journal of Child & Youth Care*, 1991, 6(1), 11-17.

Clarke, R. V., & Lester, D. *Suicide: closing the exits*. New York: Springer-Verlag, 1989.

Clum, G. A., & Lerner, M. A problem solving approach to treating individuals at risk for suicide. In D. Lester (Ed.) *Current concepts of suicide*. Philadelphia: Charles Press, 1990, 194-202.

Davenport, J. A., & Davenport, J. Native American suicide. *Social Casework*, 1987, 68, 533-539.

DeBruyn, L., Hymbaugh, K., & Valdez, N. Helping communities address suicide and violence. *American Indian & Alaska Native Mental Health Research*, 1988, 1(3), 56-65.

DeBruyn, L., Serna, P., Wilkins, B., & Nelson, S. H. In the circle of relationships. In D. Lester (Ed.) *Suicide '94*. Denver, CO: American Association of Suicidology, 1994, 39-41.

Diggory, J. Empirical evidence for the improved prediction and prevention of suicide. Pittsburgh: Chatham College, undated.

Dizmang, L. Suicide among the Cheyenne Indians. Talk given to the Los Angeles Suicide Prevention Center, 1966.

Earls, F., Escobar, J. I., & Manson, S. M. Suicide in minority groups. In S. J. Blumenthal & D. J. Kupfer (Eds.) *Suicide over the life cycle*. Washington, DC: American Psychiatric Press, 1990, 571-598.

French, L. A., & Hornbuckle, J. Indian stress and violence. *Journal of Alcohol & Drug Education*, 1979, 25, 36-43.

Hetzel, S., Winn, V., & Tolstoshev, H. Loss and change. *Journal of Adolescence*, 1991, 14, 323-334.

Jordan, J. B. Interventions with Native Americans. In D. Capuzzi & L. Golden (Eds.) *Preventing adolescent suicide*. Muncie, IN: Accelerated Development, 1988, 299-322.

Kahn, M. W., & Delk, I. L. Developing a community mental health clinic on an Indian reservation. *International Journal of Social Psychiatry*, 1973, 19, 299-306.

Kahn, M. W., Lejero, L., Antone, M., Francisco, D., & Manuel, J. An indigenous community mental health service on the Tohono O'odham (Papago) Indian Reservation. *American Journal of Community Psychology*, 1988, 16, 369-379.

Kinzie, J. D., Shore, J. H., & Pattison, E. M. Anatomy of psychiatric consultation to rural Indians. *Community Mental Health Journal*, 1972, 8, 196-207.

Kreitman, N., & Foster, J. The construction and selection of predictive scales, with special reference to parasuicide. *British Journal of Psychiatry*, 1991, 159, 185-192.

LaFromboise, T. D., & Howard-Pitney, B. The Zuni life skills development curriculum. *American Indian & Alaska Native Mental Health Research*, 1994, 4, monograph, 98-121.

Lester, D. Attempts to predict suicidal risk using psychological tests. *Psychological Bulletin*, 1970, 74, 1-17.

Lester, D. Experience of personal loss and later suicide. *Acta Psychiatrica Scandinavica*, 1989, 79, 450-452.

Lester, D. *Why people kill themselves*. Springfield, IL: Charles Thomas, 1992.

Lester, D., & Danto, B. *Suicide behind bars*. Philadelphia: Charles Press, 1993.

Levy, J. E. The effects of labeling on health behavior and treatment programs among North American Indians. *American Indian & Alaska Native Mental Health Research*, 1988, 1, monograph 1, 211-231.

Levy, J. E., & Kunitz, S. J. A suicide prevention program for Hopi youth. *Social Science & Medicine*, 1987, 25, 931-940.

Long, K. A. Suicide intervention and prevention with Indian adolescent populations. *Issues in Mental Health Nursing*, 1986, 8, 247-253.

Maris, R. W., Berman, A. L., Maltsberger, J. T., & Yufit, R. I. (Eds.) *Assessment and prediction of suicide*. New York: Guilford, 1992.

May, P. Suicide and self-destruction among American Indian youths. *American Indian & Alaska Native Mental Health Research*, 1987, 1(1), 52-69.

May, P. A., & Dizmang, L. H. Suicide and the American Indian. *Psychiatric Annals*, 1974, 4(11), 22-28.

McIntosh, J. L., & Santos, J. F. Suicide counseling and intervention with racial/ethnic minorities. In C. L. Hatton & S. M. Valente (Eds.) *Suicide assessment and intervention*. Norwalk, CT: Appleton-Century-Crofts, 1984, 175-194.

Mindell, C., & Stuart, P. Suicide and self-destructive behavior in the Oglala Sioux. *Pine Ridge Research Bulletin*, 1968, 1, 14-23.

Mindell, C., & Stuart, P. Suicide and self-destructive behavior in the Oglala Sioux. In *Suicide among the American Indians*. Washington, DC: US Department of Health, Education, & Welfare, 1969, 25-33. PHS Publication No. 1903.

Motto, J. A., Heilbron, D., & Juster, R. Development of a clinical instrument to estimate suicide risk. *American Journal of Psychiatry*, 1985, 142, 680-686.

Neligh, G. Secondary and tertiary prevention strategies applied to suicide among American Indians. *American Indian & Alaska Native Mental Health Research*, 1988, 1(3), 4-18.

Ogden, M., Spector, M. I., & Hill, C. A. Suicides and homicides among Indians. *Public Health Reports*, 1970, 85, 75-80.

Pollack, D., & Shore, J. H. Validity of the MMPI with Native Americans. *American Journal of Psychiatry*, 1980, 137, 946-950.

Prince, C. Recognition of predisposing factors which affect the high suicide rate of Canadian Indians. *Arctic Medical Research*, 1988, 47, supplement 1, 588-589.

Ratcliffe, R. W. The open door. *Lancet*, 1962, ii, 188-190.

Rhoades, E. R., Reyes, L. L., & Buzzard, G. D. The organization of health services for Indian people. *Public Health Reports*, 1987, 102, 352-356.

Rutz, W., van Knorring, L., & Walinder, J. Frequency of suicide on Gotland after systematic postgraduate education of general practitioners. *Acta Psychiatrica Scandinavica*, 1989, 80, 151-154.

Ryerson, D. Suicide awareness education in schools. In A. A. Leenaars & S. Wenckstern (Eds.) *Suicide prevention in schools*. New York: Hemisphere, 1991, 99-112.

Schifano, F., & De Leo, D. Can pharmacological intervention aid in the prevention of suicidal behavior? *Pharmacopsychiatry*, 1991, 24, 113-117.

Shaffer, D., Garland, A., Gould, M., Fisher, P., & Trautman, P. Preventing teenage suicide. *Journal of the American Academy of Child & Adolescent Psychiatry*, 1988, 27, 675-687.

Shore, J. H., Bopp, J. F., Waller, T. R., & Dawes, J. W. A suicide prevention center on an Indian reservation. *American Journal of Psychiatry*, 1972, 128, 1086-1091.

Speck, R., & Rueveni, U. Network therapy. *Family Process*, 1969, 8, 182-191.

Stack, S. Media impacts on suicide. In D. Lester (Ed.) *Current concepts of suicide*. Philadelphia: Charles Press, 1990, 107-120.

Stivers, C. Promotion of self-esteem in the prevention of suicide. In A. A. Leenaars & S. Wenckstern (Eds.) *Suicide prevention in schools*. New York: Hemisphere, 1991, 51-69.

Thompson, J. W. Prevention of adolescent suicide among American Indian and Alaskan Native peoples. In *Report of the Secretary's Task Force on Youth Suicide*. Washington, DC: U.S. Government Printing Office, 1989, Volume 3, 152-156.

Tyler, J. D., Cohen, K. N., & Clark, J. S. Providing community consultation in a reservation setting. *Journal of Rural Community Psychology*, 1982, 3(1), 49-58.

Walk, D. Suicide and community care. *British Journal of Psychiatry*, 1967, 113, 1381-1391.

Ward, J. A. Preventive implications of a Native Indian mental health program. *Journal of Preventive Psychiatry*, 1984, 2, 371-385.

Webb, J. P., & Willard, W. Six American Indian patterns of suicide. In N. L. Farberow (Ed.) *Suicide in different cultures*. Baltimore: University Park Press, 1975, 17-33.

Young, T. K., Moffatt, M. E. K., & O'Neill,. J. D. An epidemiological perspective of injuries in the Northwest Territories. *Arctic Medical Research*, 1992, 51, Supplement 7, 27-36.

Chapter 10

CONCLUSIONS

As we mentioned at the beginning of this book, suicide in American Indians causes us concern because, not only is suicidal behavior sometimes seen as an indicator that the level of psychological and psychiatric distress is high in the community, but also because the mistreatment of American Indians in the past stimulates our concern with their state today. This final chapter will review the information we have presented in this book, present some speculations about the causes of suicide in American Indians and make suggestions for future work on this topic.

THE RATE OF SUICIDE IN AMERICAN INDIANS

In recent years, say from 1945 on, the overall American Indian suicide rate has not been especially high. According to data published by the Indian Health Service (1988), the ratio of the age-adjusted American Indian suicide rate to the age-adjusted rate of other Americans was 1.2 in both 1955 and 1985, that is 20% higher than the suicide rate of other Americans. In 1985, the age-adjusted American Indian suicide rate was 14.1 per 100,000 per year and that for America as a whole 11.5. These rates should be viewed in a broader context, in which the American suicide rate is quite low as compared to countries such as Hungary with a 1980 suicide rate of 45, Denmark 29, Switzerland 25, Sri Lanka 28, and Korea 21 (Lester, 1996).

What is noteworthy in the American Indian suicide rate is the peak for young people and the trough in the elderly. For example, in 1983-1985, the suicide rate for American Indian males aged 15 to 24 years was 45.1 and for males 75 to 84 years of age 3.7 (Indian Health Service, 1988). This peak in the suicide rate for the youth (which is found also in American Indian females) is found in other subcultures, such as Australian aborigines and Pacific islanders. It is also found in some underdeveloped nations.

In Chapter 3, we noted some important questions which can be asked about this peak in American Indian suicide rates among youth. Is it found in both urbanized and reservation youth, and on all reservations or only on some? Has the peak changed over the years -- is it getting more or less pronounced?

This rise in youth suicide rates has been noted in many nations of the world in recent years (Lester, 1988a), and there are few clues as to what differentiates between those nations which have experienced a rising youth suicide rate and those which have not. In some nations such as Canada (Leenaars and Lester, 1992), the youth suicide rate is now almost as high as the suicide rate for elderly males, while in others, such as America, the youth suicide rate now appears as a secondary peak.

Thus, this peak in American Indian suicide rates may be a reflection of a phenomenon which is world-wide. If so, then possible explanations for the high suicide rate in American Indian youth may differ from those which might apply if it were a unique phenomenon.

Furthermore, we do not know whether it is the high suicide rate in American Indian youth which is noteworthy from a theoretical perspective or the low suicide rate in elderly American Indians. If we argue, for example, that the conditions of American Indians, especially on reservations, are poor, then we might predict high suicide rates for American Indians of all ages. Why then do the elderly American Indians have low suicide rates? Perhaps the anomaly lies in the elderly?

Although we have noted that suicide is often used an indicator of the level of psychological and psychiatric distress in a community, there are theories which have taken the opposite perspective. For example, Lester (1988b) has argued that suicide might be a symptom of modern society and that suicide rates will increase as the conditions of life improve. Lester argued that the high suicide rates in youth around the world in recent years could be a result of the improvement in their living conditions. Perhaps it is only when life is materially improved that we have the time and motivation to worry about existential issues such as whether life is worth living and whether we should continue to live. After all, those living through wars and famines appear, as far as we can tell, to fight for and to cling to life at all costs.

Seiden's (1981) speculations of why elderly American Indians have a low suicide rate (Chapter 5) are pertinent in this context. His paper takes the position that this is the phenomenon to be explained rather than the high youth suicide rates. Taking the traditional view that suicide is a sign of distress in the society, he argues that elderly American Indians may be in less distress than the younger adult -- they may have more prestige, they have come to terms with the culture conflict, the violence-prone are already dead, etc.

The relative cohort-size hypothesis is also relevant here (Chapter 5). This hypothesis argues that when the size of a birth cohort is large, then the members of this birth cohort will face increased competition for the finite resources available and there will not be enough to go around. Thus, the level of psychological distress will be high. Since the American Indian population has a large youth cohort, this hypothesis would predict a high youth suicide rate. For example, in 1980, 55% of the American Indian population was under the age of 25 as compared to 41% of the total American population (Indian Health Service, 1988) and, as most commentators point out, there are fewer opportunities and resources for American Indian youth than for American youth in general because of the poverty and lack of resources on most reservations. Despite the attractiveness of the cohort size hypothesis, there has been no research to test its applicability to American Indian youth suicide rates.

Lester and Uematsu (Lester, 1992) have proposed a hypothesis that each birth cohort has only a limited number of suicidal individuals. Therefore, if a birth cohort has a high suicide rate at one point in its life, then it will have a low suicide rate at other times. The phenomenon of high American Indian youth suicide rates, therefore, leads to a prediction from Lester and Uematsu's theory that these birth cohorts will have low suicide rates later in life since the majority of the suicidal individuals will already have died. Again, this hypothesis (which is similar to one of the possible explanations proposed by Seiden for the low elderly suicide rate) is worthy of empirical testing.

Finally, the finding by Levy (1988), discussed in Chapter 9, that completed suicides among the Shoshoni-Bannock were found in only eight of the families, illustrates the importance of good epidemiological research and raises questions about the appropriateness of typical suicide prevention efforts. The existence of such a pattern suggests either the presence of a genetically transmitted affective disorder in the families or learning in the families (or both), and it suggests intensive intervention with those families rather than a more broad-based suicide prevention effort. However, Levy did warn about the dangers of stigmatizing these families further through labeling them in the course of treatment, and Lester (1989) has suggested that such labeling may increase the risk of suicide, at least for some individuals. Levy's finding also raises the question of whether this phenomenon (of suicides clustering in only a few families) is found in other American Indian tribes also, a question that has not yet been explored.

Psychological Factors in American Indian Suicide

The most noteworthy finding from our review of psychological factors in American Indian suicide is that the same variables which predict suicidal behavior in all of the nations of the world which have been studied also predict suicide in American Indians, variables such as depression, hopelessness, stress, and psychiatric disorder. Although some investigators have proposed other variables which may be important for understanding American Indian suicide, such as acculturation stress and American Indian attitudes, no study has yet operationalized these variables and sought to examine their relevance for American Indian suicide empirically.

This omission is, in some ways, a great pity. There are some who argue that American Indian suicide is unique, that the causes of suicidal behavior in this group are different from the causes of suicidal behavior in the dominant culture, for example, and therefore merit special study. The results at present do not support this position. To recapitulate just one study, Dinges and Quang (1994) found that suicidal ideation in American Indian boarding school students was predicted by gender, depression scores, alcohol and drug use, somatic symptoms and family cohesion. Results such as these are reported regularly in studies of suicidal ideation in students of all ethnic groups and nationalities. For example, Slap, et al. (1989) found that attempted suicide in adolescents was predicted by gender, psychiatric disturbance, recent stress, alcohol and drug abuse, and worse family relationships.

Furthermore, the results of studies on non-American Indian adolescents show great variation, and so the absence of a particular correlate in a study on American Indian youths is not critical. For example, De Wilde, et al. (1994), in a study of Dutch youth, found that prior suicidal preoccupation was associated with current suicidal risk, while alcohol and drug abuse and recent stress were not. Thus, a small discrepancy between a study on American Indian adolescents and a study on Anglo students may not be of great importance and outweighed by the fact that the same variables come up again and again as useful for predicting suicidal behavior in adolescents and adults around the world.

Thus, a decision as to whether American Indian suicidal behavior is caused by identical psychological factors as suicidal behavior in other cultures cannot be made conclusively at the present time. The tentative answer appears to in the affirmative, but a definitive answer must await the construction of psychological tests to measure variables such as acculturation stress which have been proposed as pertinent to American Indian suicidal behavior.

Finally, although acculturation stress was often mentioned by commentators on American Indian suicide, the empirical data presented were usually irrelevant to the role of acculturation. Thus, the role of acculturation stress remains unproven. Indeed Berlin (1986) presented case histories where stress resulted from the American Indian community pressuring its members to not leave and to not achieve success in the larger society, rather than the stress on the American Indian from the larger society after he or she has moved off the reservation.

SOCIOLOGICAL STUDIES OF THE CAUSES OF AMERICAN INDIAN SUICIDE

A review of the research on sociological theories of suicide in Chapter 5 indicated that both acculturation and Durkheim's theory of social integration/regulation may be useful in accounting for the regional and tribal variation in American Indian suicide rates. Comparisons of the suicide rates of the Apache, Navajo and Pueblo in New Mexico by May and Van Winkle indicated that a moderate amount of social integration and a low level of acculturation might be associated with a low suicide rate. However, better sociological research would use a large sample of regions or tribes and, apart from Bachman's (1992) study, this has not yet been done.

The discrepant results on the variation of suicide rates with geographic isolation from Alberta and Manitoba (with the isolated communities having higher suicide rates in Alberta and lower suicide rates in Manitoba) indicate that the role of acculturation in determining American Indian suicide rates may be not be uniform or simple.

It should be noted that the variables which account for the variation in suicide rates between the different American Indian tribes may differ from those variables which explain the difference in suicide rates between American Indians and the other ethnic groups in America.

What is needed in these sociological studies of suicide in American Indian tribes is better and more extensive measures of relevant variables. For example, Van Winkle and May (1986) reported crude suicide rates for 1957-1979 of 43.3 for Apache, 27.8 for the Pueblo and 12.0 for the Navajo. In another study, May, et al. (1983) reported the incidence of fetal alcohol syndrome in these three tribes for 1980-1982: Apache (and Ute) 9.8, Pueblo

2.0 and Navajo 1.4 per 1,000 births. These three rates are in the same order as the three suicide rates. Thus, if we use the incidence of fetal alcohol syndrome as an indicator of the level of alcohol abuse in the society, we can see that the societies with more alcohol abuse had higher suicide rates. Thus, we might conclude that societal rates of alcohol abuse predict, and perhaps cause, societal rates of suicide. Of course, a sample size of three societies is much too small for reliable conclusions to be drawn, but this does illustrate the kinds of data and studies we need to pursue sociological explanations of tribal suicide rates.

To give another example, in earlier chapters, behaviors such as physical and sexual abuse of children was proposed as a cause of the high American Indian youth suicide rate. Hypotheses such as these need to be tested empirically using an adequate sample of American Indian tribes to see whether they have merit.

Finally, the suggestion by Bachman (1992) that American Indian violence is more balanced between inward-directed violence (suicide) and outward-directed violence (homicide) than is the case for African Americans and white Americans is provocative and worthy of further investigation. Is this balance characteristic of all American Indian tribes or only some? Has it always been true and will it continue to be true? The style of directing violence is an important phenomenon for cross-cultural study.

PREVENTING AMERICAN INDIAN SUICIDE

In Chapter 9, we reviewed the reports of programs to prevent suicide among American Indians, and there have been a good number of projects set up and described in the scholarly literature. However, there has been virtually no evaluation of these programs, and so we cannot be sure that these programs are having an impact on the suicidal and other pathological behaviors in the communities served. This must be remedied in the future, and evaluation must accompany these suicide prevention efforts.

Some further comments are warranted here. First, almost all of the suicide prevention efforts have been focused on American Indians living on reservations. American Indians who have moved to non-reservation areas have been ignored, with rare exceptions (such as Westermeyer [1979]).

Second, the consensus is that suicide prevention on the reservations should be carried out by American Indians. It appears from the reports that it has been difficult to find trained staff to take over the administrative and professional roles in these services. The programs typically start by using American Indian staff in paraprofessional roles. In time, hopefully, more and more American Indians will obtain the skills necessary to take over the higher level roles.

This consensus does have the implication, however, that American Indians should remain on the reservation. Certainly, American Indians should have the right and ability to remain on the reservation should they choose to do so. But we are presented with an interesting dilemma. Some American Indian reservations have a high suicide rate, yet the overall American Indian suicide is not much higher than that for the total population. The implication here is that American Indians who have moved into the mainstream society do not experience a high suicide rate. This is only an implication, and epidemiological research to examine the accuracy of this implication is needed.

The question is, therefore, from a mental health point of view, whether American Indians should be encouraged to leave reservations. In Chapter 5, we presented a couple of cases of American Indians who were successful in their education efforts and who experienced great pressure from their American Indian communities to not go on to graduate school, pressure that led to suicidal behavior in one case (Berlin, 1986). Such attitudes on the part of the American Indian community are oppressive for the individual. Given that American Indians were settled on land that does not present the best opportunities for setting up industries, it seems unfair to pressure those who could leave and be successful in the larger society to remain on the reservations. All other ethnic groups in America have, on the whole, tried to join and achieve success in the larger society. Why encourage one ethnic group to be different and to remain apart from the larger society. It may be argued that it is important for American Indians to maintain their traditional and cultural customs, but other ethnic groups have managed to preserve some of their heritage while participating in the modern world.

There is the tendency to see less developed societies as somehow better than modern society, a belief akin to the myth of the "noble savage." This is a myth (Walter, 1994-1995) and, for American Indians in particular, MacAndrew and Edgerton (1969) noted physical and psychological abuse of many kinds in their societies, including brutality, slavery, human sacrifice, ritual orgies, prostitution, and cannibalism. At present, there seems to be a tendency to view traditional methods of healing as better suited to American Indians than modern methods. I prefer modern methods, and I certainly demand the right to have access to them if I choose, as well as keeping the right to choose alternative methods if I want to. I do not grant the power to someone else to choose the methods for me.

As we mentioned in Chapter 5, there has been criticism of adoption of American Indian children by non-American Indian families and recommendations to move such children back to American Indian communities (Connors, 1996). Yet this is not the recommendation typically made for children from other nations, such as Korea, who may experience problems as they grow up in America.

The role of acculturation stress has not been sufficiently well documented for American Indians yet for us to draw definite conclusions, but it would seem important, after it has been documented and studied in greater detail, to develop strategies for easing the stress from acculturation for those American Indians who want to acculturate, while also preserving the possibility of not acculturating for those who decline to do so. Much of the writing on this problem, however, seems biased by the position that American Indians should remain on the reservation and that acculturation is bad. The implied solution is to improve conditions on the reservation rather than helping American Indians move off the reservation. To take an analogy, the solution for immigrants to America who experience acculturation stress is to support them in settling down here rather than urging them to return to their home countries.

Clearly each American Indian should be free to make his or her choice and should receive help in making that choice. Many of the reports reviewed here appear to have adopted the strategy of improving life on the reservation. More efforts should be made to provide American Indians with support and counseling to pursue whatever path they choose -- making life better for those who choose to stay on the reservation and supporting those who choose to leave.

There seems general agreement that some of those providing this counseling and support should be American Indians so that American Indians in distress can choose counselors from their own ethnic group if they so desire. I have used the phrase "some of those" since it is wrong to assume that all members of an ethnic group want to go to counselors of their same ethnic identity. This is not so, and Sue and Sue (1990) presented the case of a Chinese American who resented being assigned to a Chinese-American counselor.

What we might recommend for the individual's psychological health may come into conflict with social and political pressures from the American Indian community and from the larger society. There are, after all, social and political factors affecting decisions made concerning American Indians. It would be welcome if more psychologists and psychiatrists participated in these decisions, professionals who might be expected to weigh more strongly the psychological needs of individuals.

Finally, the quality of life of American Indians living on reservations needs to be improved. However, from a suicidological perspective, there is good evidence cross-nationally that suicide rates are higher in those nations with a higher quality of life (Lester, 1989). Therefore, public health officials should not be surprised if the improvement of material conditions does not automatically lead to an improvement in American Indian suicide rates. It may, but such an improvement would be inconsistent with the cross-national results.

REFERENCES

Bachman, R. *Death and violence on the reservation*. New York: Auburn House, 1992.

Berlin, I. Psychopathology and its antecedents among American Indian adolescents. *Advances in Clinical Child Psychology*, 1986, 9, 125-152.

Connors, E. A. The healing path. In A. A. Leenaars & D. Lester (Eds.) *Suicide and the unconscious*. Northvale, NJ: Jason Aronson, 1996, 259-269.

De Wilde, E. J., Kienhorst, C. W. M., Diekstra, R. F. W., & Wolters, W. H. G. Social support, life events, and behavioral characteristics of psychologically distressed adolescents at high risk for attempting suicide. *Adolescence*, 1994, 29, 49-60.

Dinges, N. G., & Quang, D. T. Suicide ideation and suicide attempts among American Indian and Alaska Native boarding school adolescents. *American Indian & Alaska Native Mental Health Research*, 1994, 4, monograph, 167-188.

Indian Health Service. *Chart series book*. Washington, DC: US Government Printing Office, 1988.

Leenaars, A. A., & Lester, D. Comparison of rates and patterns of suicide in Canada and the United States, 1960-1988. *Death Studies*, 1992, 16, 417-430.

Lester, D. Youth suicide. *Adolescence*, 1988a, 23, 955-958.

Lester, D. One theory of teenage suicide. *Journal of School Health*, 1988b, 58, 193-194.

Lester, D. *Suicide from a sociological perspective*. Springfield, IL: Charles Thomas, 1989.

Lester, D. *Why people kill themselves*. Springfield, IL: Charles Thomas, 1992.

Lester, D. *Patterns of suicide and homicide in the world*. Commack, NY: Nova Science, 1996.

MacAndrew, C., & Edgerton, R. B. *Drunken comportment*. Chicago: Aldine, 1969.

May, P. A., Hymbach, K. T., Aase, J. M., & Samet, J. M. Epidemiology of fetal alcohol syndrome among American Indians of the southwest. *Social Biology*, 1983, 30, 374-387.

Slap, G. B., Vorters, D. F., Chaudhuri, S., & Cantor, R. M. Risk factors for attempted suicide during adolescence. *Pediatrics*, 1989, 84, 762-772.

Sue, D. W., & Sue, D. *Counseling the culturally different*. New York: Wiley, 1990.

Van Winkle, N. W., & May, P. A. Native American suicide in New Mexico, 1957-1979. *Human Organization*, 1986, 45, 296-309.

Walker, T. Natural death and the noble savage. *Omega*, 1994-1995, 30, 237-248.

Westermeyer, J. Ethnic identity problems among ten Indian psychiatric patients. *International Journal of Social Psychiatry*, 1979, 25, 188-197.

INDEX

P

Q

R

S